Bags That Rock

Knitting on the Road with
KELLEY DEAL

LARK BOOKS

A Division of Sterling Publishing Co., Inc.
New York / London

DEVELOPMENT EDITOR: **SUZANNE J. E. TOURTILLOTT**
EDITOR: **NATHALIE MORNU**
ART DIRECTOR: **KRISTI PFEFFER**
COVER DESIGNER: **CHRIS BRYANT & CHRIS GLASS**
ILLUSTRATORS: **ORRIN LUNDGREN AND EVA REITZEL**
PHOTOGRAPHER: **STEWART O'SHIELDS**

Dedication

For my mother

Library of Congress Cataloging-in-Publication Data

Deal, Kelley.
  Bags that rock : knitting on the road / with Kelley Deal. -- 1st ed.
    p. cm.
  Includes index.
  ISBN-13: 978-1-60059-158-7 (pb-trade pbk. : alk. paper)
  ISBN-10: 1-60059-158-2 (pb-trade pbk. : alk. paper)
  1. Knitting--Patterns. 2. Handbags. I. Title.
  TT825.D42 2008
  746.43'2041--dc22

                              2008001464

10 9 8 7 6 5 4 3 2 1

First Edition

Published by Lark Books, A Division of
Sterling Publishing Co., Inc.
387 Park Avenue South, New York, NY 10016

Text © 2008, Kelley Deal
Photography © 2008, Lark Books unless otherwise specified
Illustrations © 2008, Lark Books

Distributed in Canada by Sterling Publishing,
c/o Canadian Manda Group, 165 Dufferin Street
Toronto, Ontario, Canada M6K 3H6

Distributed in the United Kingdom by GMC Distribution Services,
Castle Place, 166 High Street, Lewes, East Sussex, England BN7 1XU

Distributed in Australia by Capricorn Link (Australia) Pty Ltd.,
P.O. Box 704, Windsor, NSW 2756 Australia

If you have questions or comments about this book, please contact:
Lark Books
67 Broadway
Asheville, NC 28801
828-253-0467

Manufactured in China

ISBN 13: 978-1-60059-158-7

For information about custom editions, special sales, and premium
and corporate purchases, please contact the Sterling Special Sales
Department at 800-805-5489, or specialsales@sterlingpub.com.

Somewhere in Europe...

... I learned to knit. I was on tour in the '90s and the German girlfriend of the opening band's drummer taught me how. My first project was a sweater. It was un-wearable—I think I had a sleeve coming out of the back and I didn't finish it—but I became addicted! After my first Frankensweater, I knit a series of too-short sweaters in the most ghastly colors of acrylic yarns. They only looked good on our drummer, Nick.

Many sweaters later, my roommate, Alex, had a birthday coming up, so I started experimenting with knitted handbags. I made one after another until I had an entire collection. On the advice of friends, I started selling my creations in boutiques in Minneapolis, where I lived at the time. For me, handbags are the perfect project: it's easy to travel with knitting tools and supplies, and bags are fast to make. Knitted bags are more than just sewn-together knitted squares; they're cool little pieces of art.

In this book you're going to find a wide variety of bags, many felted, some not. The Trixie Delicious (page 110) is so elegant it looks like it came from a boutique, but even a first-time knitter can pull it off. With its structured shape, the Road bag (page 64) is a great everyday tote because it can handle a lot of punishment and you can stuff tons of junk in it. The unique Telephone bag (page 36) has a handle that makes me laugh, and every time people see it, they just have to touch it.

Most of the designs and techniques you'll find here are simple, and don't require much beyond the skills of a beginner. Most of the basic components are squares or rectangles, which are easy to knit and purl. When you're ready for a challenge, you can try trickier techniques such as the simple shaping on The Tube bag (page 50), or knitting blocks of color, as done on the Laura Petrie (page 44). You'll learn how to felt (I explain my super-easy washing-machine method), and what kinds of yarns and needles work best if you'd rather not felt at all. I explore fibers of all kinds—including

"All the cool women knit:
Emmylou Harris,
Eleanor Roosevelt,
Miss Marple."

some that you might not think to knit with. The Sari bag (page 84), using deluxe yarn made from the mill ends of silk saris, is an explosion of color. And why stop shopping for fiber just because you've left the yarn store? I made the Hey, Jute bag (page 90) out of a vegetable fiber cord I bought in a hardware store. I'll also show you some secrets for finding and using bag hardware that makes a handmade purse look really pulled together.

As a bonus, every project is accompanied by Remix options that can take a bag's style in totally unique directions, with suggestions for changing yarns and colors, creating and improvising handles, and using funky embellishments both found and made. The same basic design for the felted Heart bag (page 78), for example, can look girly knitted up in red with a little skeleton key dangling from its tip, or get Remixed goth-style in black yarn, decorated with a charm in the shape of handcuffs.

Whether on tour or in the studio, I always make time to shop for yarn and try new fibers. This book is a reflection of what I've learned through experience and experimentation over the years, and I've included some photos and stories about knitting on the road. I hope these pages inspire and encourage fellow knitters to experiment. Be creative with the concept of a boring old square, and turn it into your own little work of art.

All the cool women knit: Emmylou Harris, Eleanor Roosevelt, Miss Marple. Being in the recording studio can be a really stressful time. There's a lot of waiting around, and self-doubt can plague you. Yet I saw Emmylou in a Gram Parsons documentary, yarn and needles in hand— perfectly at peace. She seemed confident and exuded a grace that I've associated with knitting ever since. Knitting keeps me occupied and serene whether I'm riding in a tour bus, waiting on an airplane, or obsessing in the studio.

My knitting shelves... jealous?

Logically, the first element to consider when making a bag is the type of material you're going to use. Allow me to walk you through some fiber options, as well as some of the tools you will need to get started.

STRINGS: YARN AND FIBERS

When you make a bag the first thing you start with is a *fabric*—the knitted fibers. A nice thick fabric provides instant structure for your project. Most of the time I prefer bags that can hold their own shape but I also like the "slouch" styles too. Most of the ones you'll see in this book have very defined shapes.

A thick fabric doesn't necessarily mean you used a heavy-weight yarn. There are a couple of ways to achieve the right kind of thick fabric for a knitted bag. One of the most popular is to felt knitted wool, but your options aren't limited to that approach alone. Some yarns are sturdy enough to stand on their own. Others need nothing more than to be knitted with smallish needles to create a durable, close-weave fabric.

Felt-able

Felting is the process of matting together wool fibers (page 16). If you're new to felting you should know that not all fibers can be felted, and even so the look of the finished felt varies from one fiber to another. There are lots of different kinds of felt-able wools. Some are hairier than others, and the least "fuzzy" of them create some very crisp felts. The Propeller project on page 74 is a good example. Notice how sharp the motif's edges look? You can't get this look with a fuzzy lopi or similarly fluffy wool.

Playing Lollapalooza in the summer of 1994

Wools with a lot of *loft* (fluffy fuzziness), on the other hand, make really shaggy felts. The Edie bag on page 70 shows lopi wool at its best. When felted, the stitch definition is completely gone, and the hairy fibers create a color depth that you can't find in non-fuzzy wools. So pay attention to the yarn's label. It must say 100 percent wool (with one notable exception) and should not be a "super wash" type.

Mohair, shorn from a goat, is an extreme example of how the hair's loft increases the complexity and nuance of color. And the color selection is splendid—you can't even think of a color that isn't available in mohair. One thing: the popular brands of mohair are a blend of mohair, wool, and about nine percent nylon. So mohair is an exception to the 100-percent-wool rule, though I won't felt it if it contains any more nylon than that. Nothing looks worse than felted mohair that shows its stitch definition! When felted correctly, mohair's high density of fibers

results in a very thick durable fabric. (I'll talk more about the felting process later.)

Let me take a moment to praise the virtues of alpaca wool. Alpaca comes not from sheep or goats but from fiber animals called alpacas. When I was in L.A., selecting the yarn for the Turtleneck bag on page 96, I asked the guy in the store, "Hey, how does alpaca felt?" He looked at me like he was going to cry. He said, while petting the alpaca skein, "You can't! It's too beautiful. Look how soft!" So of course I went right home, did some knitting and washed it up, and it felts like a dream. I felted up a black and white tweed, and something about the felting process caused the two colors to combine and form a thick gray fabric with nubs and specks of black and white. Honestly, it looks like a Chanel suit. Experiment! Mix and match these yarns. Combine a strand of mohair with a strand of alpaca; mix ad infinitum. Have fun!

Notes from the Road

Felt-able yarns

Novelty yarns

Look for non-traditional fibers in hardware stores, pharmacies, or garden centers.

Novelty

Let's talk about other fibers you can use to make a thick fabric for your hand-knit bags. There's a wide assortment of novelty yarns on the market today. Eyelash, slubby, beaded, sequined, feathered, ribboned fibers—anything you can think of, they make it. The most important thing to remember when using novelty yarns is to work with multiple strands. There's one loose general rule when knitting with more than one strand of yarn that we will be ignoring! The rule suggests that when you double the yarn you should also double the needle size recommended on the yarn's label. For example, the Clutch (page 28) uses a yarn that recommends 6.5 mm (size 10.5 U.S.) needles, but my pattern calls for two strands of yarn knit on 4.5 mm (size 7 U.S.) needles. When you start adding strands of yarn and changing the needle size, the gauge information given on the yarn's label no longer applies. That's why it's important to swatch for gauge when the pattern recommends it.

Non-Traditional

But why stop shopping for knittable fibers when you leave the yarn store? What about non-traditional fibers like hemp, sisal, plastic string, jute (see the Hey, Jute bag on page 90), twine—even strips of fabric knotted together? These are all great ingredients for making a thick fabric.

Mixing, shmixing—

You can knit with almost anything.

GEAR

A plethora of gadgets are available to assist you, the knitter (some more helpful than others). Let's take a look at some basic gear you'll need to work the projects in this book, as well as some tips for traveling with your knitting.

Needles

There are three basic types of knitting needles: straight, circular, and double-pointed. They come in all sorts of materials like wood, metal, and plastic. Just try them out to find your favorites. For some projects, though, I recommend specifically using metal needles. Sometimes when I'm knitting with multiple strands of yarn on a smaller-size wooden needle, it feels like the needles may break. I've actually snapped off the end of a (wooden) needle before.

Assorted Tools

Some nice sharp scissors are a must. Practice saying this phrase: "Not with my good scissors!"

There are many different styles of row counters but they all do the same thing: help you keep track of how many rows you've knitted. I can't recommend this tool enough.

Stitch holders are really handy and look like big, non-lethal safety pins. Stitch markers can get pretty fancy; some have dangly little beads and look like jewelry but the plain little plastic rings work just fine. Knotted loops of yarn can also be used.

For knitting swatches, and for fabric that will be fitted onto a frame, have a fabric tape measure handy.

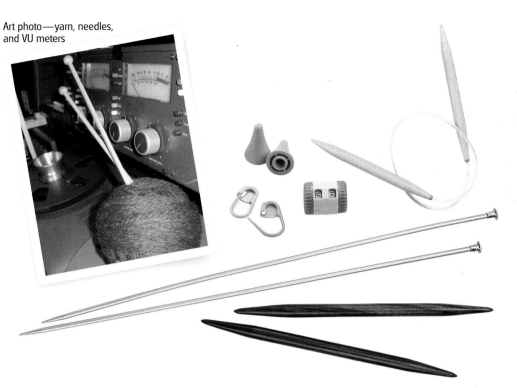

Art photo—yarn, needles, and VU meters

Tapestry needles—both those with blunt and those with sharp ends—are used to sew closures, straps, seams, and for some simple embroidery.

If you're like me, you like to keep your knitting close. Use point protectors to keep a work in progress securely on the needles.

Some knitted fabrics are finished with simple crochet stitches, so you'll need a crochet hook in a size complementary to the size of the knitting needles you've used.

Another handy tool is a dental floss threader. Instead of a needle, I thread yarn onto this simple device, and now attaching beads is a breeze. Gone are the days of searching for a needle that has an eye big enough to thread yarn through, but that's small enough to slip through the hole in a bead.

Finally, I like to have some big straight pins for positioning straps and seams before sewing.

Notes from the Road

There's a lot of downtime during a tour. I got stuck somewhere once with yarn but no needles. Luckily, The Breeders' drummer, José, had an extra pair of drumsticks. They work great in a pinch!

Some random
hotel hallway

Hardware for frames

Travel Tips

For complete information on
what you can or cannot bring in
your carry-on bag or your checked
luggage when you fly, consult
the airline's website regarding
prohibited items. Remember,
you're at the mercy of the agent
who's screening your carry-on
luggage. If the judgment call is that
your scissors or the needles pose
a threat, they can be confiscated.
Carry a self-addressed, stamped
envelope to the airport so you can
mail them to yourself. (It's mind-
boggling to me that someone could
possibly be that organized, but it
sounds like a great idea.)

And be aware that the guidelines
vary from one country to the
next. For example, even though
I've knitted on flights across the
Atlantic, I was recently relieved of
a small pair of bamboo needles on a
flight within continental Australia.
No knitting needles or scissors of
any kind are permitted in your
carry-on there.

Bag Hardware

There is such a wonderful selection
of purse hardware out there today.
The Internet is a great source
for handles, feet, closures, and
such. Look on page 127 for a note
about suppliers. Let's review
a few of the items used for the
purse projects.

Using a purse frame is an easy yet
effective method for giving shape
and structure to a bag. They're
typically made of metal and come
in various shapes. I use two types
of frames in this book, a hex-open
frame in the Clutch (page 28),
and a regular frame for the Trixie
Delicious (page 110). Simply
follow the instructions to make
the knitted fabric, then mount
the fabric to the frame with some
simple sewing.

Gauge is really important here
because your knit work must match
the frame's fixed size. Most frames
already have a pair of loops where
the ends of the strap can be easily
attached. A creative alternative to
a frame is to use metal hoops for
support; see The Tube bag on page
50 for an example. These are sewn
inside the bag after the knitting

is done.

You can use purse feet on any
bag. They protect the bottom of
the purse from dirty surfaces and
can keep a bag from tipping over.
The feet usually come in gold,
silver, or bronze, and are super-easy
to attach.

To make strap attachment
really simple, insert large eyelets,
which are typically smaller than
grommets, into the bag fabric.
Alternately, try D-rings, O-rings,
key rings, and binder rings, with
or without grommets or eyelets;
these come in a variety of colors
and sizes.

As for closures, a variety of
snaps are available: sew-on snaps,
sew-on magnetic, and magnetic
prong, just to name a few. Some
of these snaps can be visible from
the right side of your work so think
about that before you select your
snap. The bag's closure can be an
important design element of a bag.
For example, the knotted tab in
the Knotted Up bag (page 100)
echoes the knot in the strap, while
the drumsticks for the Moe bag
(page 54) play off the design of the
embroidered drums.

Bag hardware

Straps

Finding the right strap for a bag could be my favorite part of the handbag-making process. There are all kinds of things to consider. For instance, what is the weight the strap will have to bear? Will it be worn over the shoulder, or will it be hand-held? This book includes bags with designs that allow a lot of personal expression in creating and attaching a wide variety of straps.

Because a strap can completely change the look of your bag, I recommend mixing it up. Most of the strap recommendations are interchangeable. For instance, swap out the strap described in the Road bag on page 68 for the guitar string used in Graffiti, on page 114. Pay attention not only to what a strap is made of, but also how it's attached. Sometimes the process is as simple as sewing the strap directly to the bag, like on Free Bird (page 42), while in other cases I've designed the bag "strap ready" (see Road, page 64). The methods I've used to prepare the strap, and the attachment process itself, work with many different strap designs.

My goal is to provide a springboard for your imagination and to encourage you to include your hobbies and passions in personalizing a bag to make it uniquely yours.

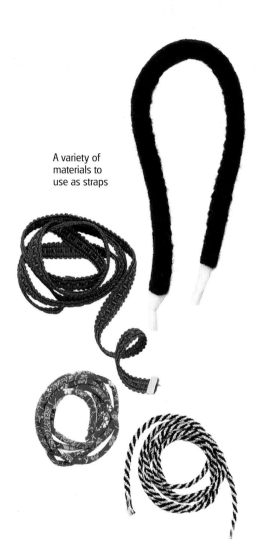

A variety of materials to use as straps

Make 'Em

A simple way to make a strap is to knit Garter Stitch to your desired length, then felt it afterwards. Using Garter Stitch will ensure that the edges won't curl (as Stockinette Stitch tends to), and the felting process prevents most stretching. Knitted I-cords, either felted or not, are also an easy option. A good way to keep a knitted strap from stretching out is to use what I call a felted tube. To do this, you knit a tube in Stockinette Stitch, as described in the Nordic bag (page 106), then stuff it with upholstery piping. The piping adds support to the strap and keeps its shape from becoming distorted. I usually sew knitted and felted straps directly onto bags.

Braiding yarn threaded with beads is a quick and simple way to make a strap for a smaller bag. Or check out The Tube bag on page 50; I used six equal lengths of strong fishing line and just loaded on the beads. Other straps you can craft yourself include other materials, such as chain, satin piping or trim, and branches. You'll find directions on how to make various straps throughout my pattern instructions.

If you add a lot of reverb when I'm sawing on the fiddle, I sound terrific!

Hunt through second-hand stores to find vintage scarves to use as straps.

Buy 'Em

Years ago I made a handle out of branches because I couldn't find an appropriate wooden handle. Today, with the Internet and the popularity of knitting, straps are falling off trees—like branches! Do some investigating: You'll discover a huge variety of purchased handles and straps for sale out there. You can buy all shapes of bamboo and wood handles, as well as acrylic or resin handles in wild, wacky colors. You'll also find beaded handles and kits for beading them yourself. Leather or vinyl straps come in over-the-shoulder styles and the hand-held variety. Again, take notice of how the strap attaches, and make sure your bag is strap-ready.

Recycle 'Em

Because it's fun to incorporate the unexpected, my favorite straps are the unusual ones. Besides, a lot of times, I just have to make do. I can't tell the bus driver, "Hey, pull over. I have to stop at a yarn store!" (The crew would kill me.) However, I can ask Mando, the bass player, to give me his old bass strings after he changes them, or ask the drummer, José, for a pair of sticks. I also like to turn form and function upside down by using necklaces, belts, scarves, telephone cord, and the inseams from an old pair of jeans as straps.

Even though I've used things like guitar strings and drum sticks as straps in this book, I include what I like to call a "civilian option" as well. Many of the patterns in this book have a Remix page that shows the bag with a more traditional strap. For example, the drumstick-handled Moe bag on page 54 looks just as cute with straight bamboo handles, as featured in its Remix section.

Unusual straps sometimes require unusual methods to attach them to a bag. The methods I describe are the easiest that I've found, but feel free to experiment.

Manny is the perfect engineer because he's always ready to lend a hand. Here we are at Sound City Studio in L.A.

Unexpected materials for straps include (clockwise from top), guitar strings, old necklaces, the inseam from a pair of jeans, and drumsticks.

SPECIAL TECHNIQUES

Let me introduce you to a few processes you might need to be familiar with as you work the projects in this book.

Felting

When hair from animals is agitated in hot, sudsy water, the rubbing together causes the fibers to knot and tangle. A piece of knitted wool will shrink to create a dense, thick fabric in which most of the stitch definition is lost. This process is known as *fulling* or (my favored term) felting. As a general rule, a knit item will lose one-third of its height and next to nothing of its width during the felting process. The bleaching process that white and lighter-colored wools undergo prevents them from felting as well as black and darker colors of yarn. Keep this in mind when selecting colors for your felted projects, and avoid mixing very light and very dark colors.

I prefer to use a washing machine for all my felting. If you haven't used a machine for felting, make sure to knit up a swatch and wash it. (If you don't own your own washer, you can definitely use one at a laundromat.) Take note of how your machine performs. It may take two or three times through the washer to get the results you want.

Start with a normal cycle set to "hot" with a medium water level. To keep your project from getting lost and to help control loose fibers that may clog up a drain, put the knitting in a washable laundry bag. (A pillowcase works great, too.) Add a couple pair of jeans to help create the agitation needed for successful felting; I don't recommend using towels, because they shed. Pour in a liberal squirt of liquid dishwashing soap, and let the knitting go through the spin cycle. Some knitters feel that doing so may cause creases in the work, but I haven't had that problem yet. Never put your felted projects in the dryer! The fibers will burn out and lose their bright colors.

Let me give you a little heads-up on something called *splaying*, which happens when the felting process widens or stretches out a bag's opening out of proportion to its base. The effect of splaying can make your project look like one of those felted hats with a brim. While those hats are quite nice, you don't want to wear your handbag on your head. You can minimize or even incorporate splaying in your project in a couple of ways.

On some projects, I tell you to cast on and knit the first four to six rows of your bag with needles that are smaller than what the project calls for. This will result in a tighter opening. I also use this technique for the last four to six rows and for the bind off.

I'm knitting in between vocal takes. Hope I got the lyrics right...

Another measure that prevents splaying involves sewing the side seams of a bag. Simply take a little more seam allowance near the top quarter of the bag.

You can also use splaying to your benefit. See the scalloped edges on the opening of the Nordic bag on page 106? Those were created because the extra felted fabric allowed me to tug and pull a shape that stayed nicely after blocking.

Blocking

The felting process will change the size of your bag and usually distorts its shape. For this reason, it's important to block felted bags. In this process, a freshly felted, malleable bag is molded around a form and allowed to dry; afterward, it retains that shape. Books are well suited for blocking molds. Just wrap a thin plastic bag around the book to protect it, and obviously don't use your first-edition *Alice in Wonderland* as a blocking mold because it may get a little damp. For non-traditional shapes, or for bags where you don't want sharp, defined edges, stuff your project to the desired shape with plastic grocery bags.

Felt once, felt twice

Take your time with the blocking process: Twist and pull your project into the shape you want. Allow it to dry completely before you work with it further. Depending on the weather, drying may take two or three days.

Hmm, 2-inch tape machine or yarn winder?

Joining Seams

If the sides of your project roll inward, give it a quick press with an iron on the appropriate heat setting. This will make sewing up the sides a lot easier. Next, pin the edges in place. Oh, quit crying—it only takes a second and will probably save you time in the long run.

I generally recommend that you use the project yarn for seaming. Exceptions are when the yarn is super bulky or a novelty yarn. For instance, the Clutch on page 28 is seamed with a flat, firm yarn in a matching color and fiber. It just makes sewing easier. The type of tapestry needle to use depends on your preferred method of sewing seams. A blunt-end needle works well with projects made from novelty yarns and bulky yarns. A sharp needle works well with projects that will be felted.

I use different methods for sewing seams, depending on the look I want to achieve, so feel free to use your preferred method. For the Trixie Delicious bag on page 110, I sewed the sides with

the right sides together using one strand of the black cotton yarn used in the project and a blunt tapestry needle. For the Hey, Jute bag on page 90, on the other hand, I sewed the edges with the wrong sides together, again with a blunt tapestry needle. This helps to support the shape and define the seams.

There are a couple projects where I chose to single crochet the sides together. This works well when using multiple strands of extra bulky yarn.

Shaping and Lining

Typically, a bag's shape is some take on sewn-together squares or rectangles. There's nothing wrong with that. It's traditional and it's functional. Usually, such designs are also the easiest to make. The trick is to give these knitted bags a sense of uniqueness and even, dare I say, artistic flair. In this book you'll find several projects that use the basic square-ish shape.

Non-traditional shapes such as cylinders and hearts are a little

more difficult, because they require some increasing or decreasing of stitches, and using double-pointed or circular needles. Such methods aren't hard, but they aren't beginner techniques either.

You'll notice I'm not afraid of sewing up seams. Seams add instant support, keeping a bag from sinking, stretching, or otherwise distorting. They're also typically a great place to attach straps.

And a note about linings. In my travels—literally around the world—visiting yarn stores and talking to other knitters, I've come to realize this truth: Knitters like to knit, but they don't like to sew. Therefore, I've designed my bags without linings. If you like to sew, feel free to line away. Or check with your favorite local yarn store. They most likely can provide a lining service for a reasonable charge.

Block this.

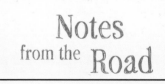

Notes
from the Road

I was stuck with a bunch of white yarn but I wanted orange and couldn't get to a yarn store. The solution? Walk to the local convenience store and get orange Kool-Aid. It makes a great cold-water dye in a pinch.

Making I-Cord

I find knitting hundreds of 4-stitch rows thankless and yawn-inducing. If you're like me and find making I-cords tedious, check out the sidebar below where my sister, Kim, reviews an automatic I-cord maker I discovered and gives a few tips for the beginner. This little machine is quite the contraption. After doing one test cord on it, I felt confident that I knew how to use it. It makes long lengths of I-cord in minutes! Kim—a novice knitter—used it to make the I-cords you see in this book.

However, I-cord can also be knitted by hand. Here's how.

With double-pointed needles, cast on the desired number of stitches. *Knit one row. Don't turn your work. Slide your work from the left end of the needle to the right end (your working yarn will be hanging from the "wrong" side). Pull it tightly in back of your work in preparation to knit another row (figure 1). Repeat from * for the desired length.

The I-cord machine.

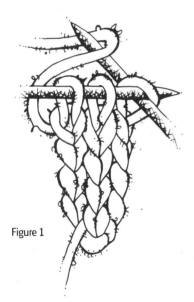

Figure 1

I-Cord Interview

Kelley: Hi, Kim! Did you find the instructions for the machine thorough and easy to follow?

Kim: Yes, although I didn't really trust the instructions at first. I looked at the diagram and thought, "Really, I'm supposed to hook one but then skip one and then hook the next one and then skip the next one?" Well, now I see that's the beginning knot. It works—just follow the diagram. I had to literally cut out my first couple of tries because the work got knotted up in the machine. I just started again and with a little practice it worked great.

Kelley: Do you have any helpful tips?

Kim: Make sure that each latched hook actually unlatches and drops the stitch off its arm. This is a simple machine to work, but I had to keep my eye on each stitch.

Kelley: How do you get the work off the machine?

Kim: Well, Kelley, they show you how in the instructions, but I tended to lose the loops if I wound the entire work off the machine. So I hooked each stitch off while the work was still on the maker, then pulled my work up and out of the machine. I didn't just wind the work off into my lap. That way, my threaded needle could go right through the loops.

Kelley: I'm sure the readers will find this very helpful. Thanks, Kim! Call me later…

Me and my sister, Kim (she's at the left), in front of Andrea's truck. This picture was taken at El Capiro's in East Los Angeles.

SPECIAL STITCHES

The project instructions will refer you back to these special knitting, crochet, and embroidery stitches. There's nothing tricky here, but you may need to practice first.

Knit

For even the simplest projects in this book, you'll need to already know how to cast on, knit, purl, and bind off. Here are methods for increasing and decreasing that you should find helpful when shaping your knit pieces.

Increasing (Inc)

Two common increase methods are used in this book: make 1 (m1), and work 2 stitches into one stitch (kfb or pfb).

Make 1 (m1)

An additional stitch can be worked into the horizontal strand between stitches. Using the left needle, and working from the front, lift the strand between stitches onto the left needle, then knit into the back of this loop.

Knit (or Purl) in Front and Back Loops (kfb or pfb)

Another common increasing method is to knit (or purl) twice into the same stitch. Knit (or purl) into a stitch normally but *don't* slip the stitch off of the needle (figure 2 and figure 4). Knit (or purl) into the back loop of the same stitch (figure 3 and figure 5). Now slip the stitch off the needle. You have worked 2 stitches into one stitch.

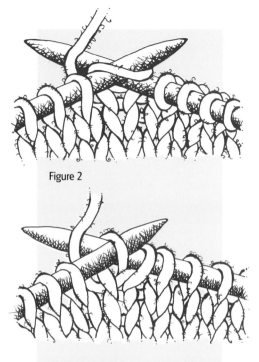

Figure 2

Figure 3

Knitting in Front and Back Loops

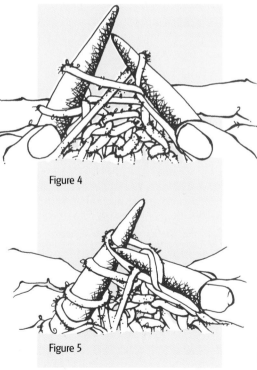

Figure 4

Figure 5

Purling in Front and Back Loops

Decreasing (Dec)

Two common decrease methods are used in this book: work 2 stitches together (k2tog or p2tog), and slip, slip, knit (ssk).

Knit (or Purl) 2 Stitches Together (k2tog or p2tog)

To knit (or purl) 2 stitches together, insert the right needle into the front loops of 2 stitches knitwise (or purlwise) at the same time. Wrap the yarn around the needle as usual and complete the stitch, slipping both stitches off the left needle. This decrease slants the stitches to the right on the knit side of the work.

Slip, slip, knit (ssk)

This is a variation of the standard decrease (k2tog) and slants the stitches to the left on the knit side of the work. Slip two stitches knitwise, one at a time, from the left needle to the right needle (figure 6). Insert the left needle into the front loops of the slipped stitches and knit them together (figure 7).

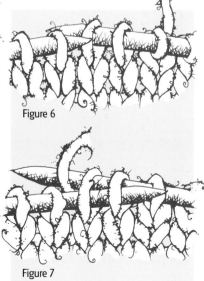

Figure 6

Figure 7

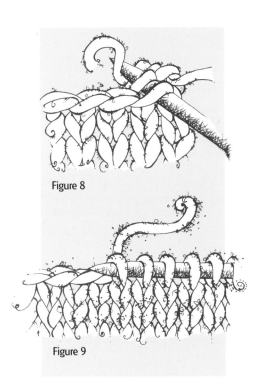

Figure 8

Figure 9

Picking Up Stitches

To pick up stitches along a horizontal bound-off edge, insert your knitting needle into the first stitch that you are working with in the row below the bound-off edge (figure 8). Wrap your yarn knitwise around the needle and draw your yarn through (figure 9). This is one stitch. Continue along until the required number of stitches is picked up.

Crochet

In this book I use single crochet in three different ways. For the Easy Evening bag (page 24), I crocheted along the finished bag opening. In the Knotted Up bag on page 100, I crocheted along the row edge of knitting. Both the Loopy (page 60) and the Telephone (page 36) patterns use crochet for sewing up the side seams.

There are three simple stitches you will need know. Yarn is joined to a knit piece with a slip stitch. Start with a slip knot on the crochet hook. Insert the hook, from front to back, into the first knit stitch you want to work. Wrap the yarn around the hook, from back to front, and draw the loop through the knit stitch and the loop on the hook so that only one loop remains on the hook.

After joining the yarn, or when beginning a new row of crochet stitches, you may need to work chain stitches. There will already be a loop on the hook. *Wrap the yarn around the hook, from back to front, and draw it through the loop on the hook.* You have completed one chain stitch and now have one loop on your hook. Continue from * to * to work as many chain stitches as desired.

You can work single crochet stitches after working a chain stitch or you can start with a slip knot on the crochet hook. *Insert the crochet hook, from front to back, into the stitch you want to work. Wrap the yarn around the hook, from back to front, and draw it through. There should be two loops on your hook (figure 10). Wrap the yarn around the hook again and draw it through these two loops.* You will now have one loop on your hook. You have completed one single crochet stitch. Continue from * to * as desired (figure 11).

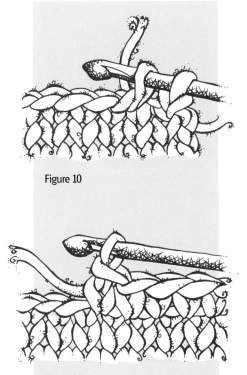

Figure 10

Figure 11

Embroidery

Embroidery adds another dimension to your knitting and can be worked on felted projects, before or after felting, as well as on non-felted projects.

Duplicate Stitch

Just like the name says, Duplicate Stitch is worked right over an existing knit stitch. Use a blunt end tapestry needle to avoid splitting the yarn strands as you work. Bring the needle up through the stitch below the one you want to cover. Tracing the V shape of the stitch, insert the needle under the two loops of the stitch above it (figure 12). Then, insert the needle back into the stitch below.

Figure 12

Back Stitch

In this book, the Back Stitch is used to embroider designs on bags that have already been felted. Using a sharp tapestry needle threaded with the project yarn and working from the right side of the bag to the left, bring the needle up through the felted fabric along the design line. Insert the needle a stitch length behind where the yarn emerged, then bring the needle back up a stitch length in front of where the yarn emerged (figure 13).

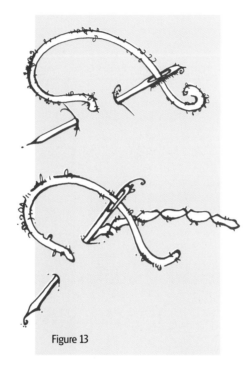

Figure 13

Split Stitch

The Split Stitch is an embroidery stitch that I use for outlines. Using a sharp tapestry needle and the project yarn, bring the needle up through the knitted fabric. Working from left to right, insert the needle a stitch away from where the yarn emerged, making a single stitch. Bring it back up in the middle of this straight stitch, splitting the yarn (figure 14). Continue working in this manner.

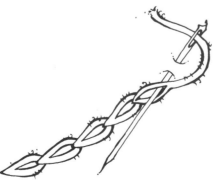

Figure 14

Blanket Stitch

I use this stitch along an edge to give a nice finish. Secure the yarn to the back of the piece and work from left to right with the edge facing you. Insert the needle down through the felted fabric a stitch away from the edge. Before pulling the yarn tight, insert the needle over the yarn and then pull to secure the stitch (figure 15). Repeat all around. Connect the last and first stitches and secure the ends.

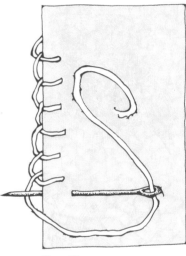

Figure 15

CUE THE SMOKE MACHINE

Okay, you've got your fiber, your gear, and your special techniques. That's enough talking—let's get knitting! The projects that follow offer lots of options, so feel free to mix it up.

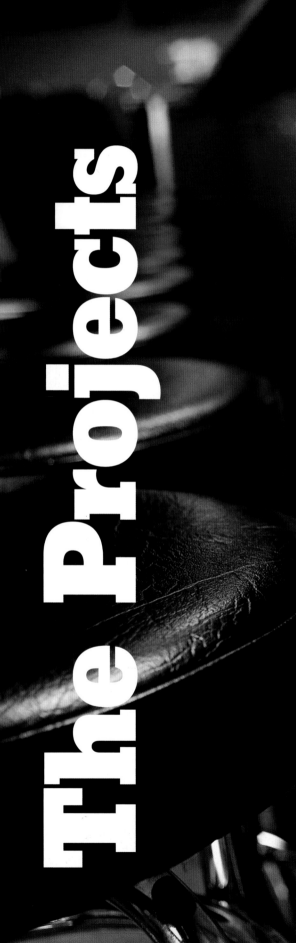

The Projects

Easy Evening

RIFF

**So easy, so fast, so shiny. Be creative with the strap!
If you don't have access to musical hardware, check
the Remix to see a necklace used for a strap.**

FINISHED MEASUREMENTS

Height of Bag: 6½"/17cm, excluding strap

Width of Bag: 5½"/14cm

MATERIALS AND TOOLS

170yd/156m of **4** worsted weight yarn, rayon blend, in silver metallic

Knitting needles: 3.75 mm (size 5 U.S.)

Pins

Blunt tapestry needle for sewing

3mm (size D-3 U.S.) crochet hook

Wire cutters or scissors

Guitar string, medium gauge, low E

2 crimps

Pliers or crimpers

2 drum lug casings

Play foam, re-moldable sculpting beads

Sew-on snap

GAUGE

Exact gauge is not essential for this project.

Knitting

Hold two strands together throughout.

Cast on 35 sts. Leave long tail for sewing.

Work in Stockinette Stitch for 110 rows.

Bind off. Leave long tail for sewing.

Assembling

Using an iron on rayon setting, press the bag to prevent rolling.

With knit sides together, pin side edges of bag together. Using tapestry needle and long tails, sew side seams. Weave in ends.

Using the crochet hook and holding two strands of yarn together, join yarn with a slip stitch in opening edge of bag and chain 1. Single crochet (page 20) around the opening edge of the bag.

Preparing the Strap

Using the wire cutters or scissors, trim the ends of the guitar string. You will be working with just the wire.

Fold one end of the wire approx 1½"/3.8cm from the end, creating a loop. Pinch the loop in place. Slip the loop through the crimp to the end of the looped wire and using pliers or crimper, crimp to secure in place. See page 15 for photograph of assembly. Do not repeat this for the other end yet.

Load up the wire as follows; slip one drum lug casing right side up onto guitar string. Then, slip second lug casing upside down on string.

Fold and crimp the other end of the guitar string.

Finishing

Using the tapestry needle and two strands held together, sew the strap edges to the inside side seams—so the bottom of the loop is approx 3½"/9cm down from the top edge of the bag. Weave in ends.

Because the holes of the lug casings are larger than the guitar string, use the play foam, re-moldable sculpting beads and fill the holes. This will prevent the lug from spinning around freely on the guitar string.

Sew on snap.

This Easy Evening bag was knit with:

2 skeins of Berroco Metallic FX, worsted weight, 85% rayon/15% metallic, 7/8oz/25g = approx 85yd/78m per skein, color #1002

Feedback

Personalized tags can give your bag a professional finish. Have them made for you, or make them yourself with ribbon and embroidery floss. This tag is a piece of ribbon with a K embroidered on it using Back Stitch (page 21).

Easy Evening REMIX

Use gold metallic yarn with a necklace for the strap.

Clutch

This bag has a retro feel...maybe because back in the day ladies weren't expected to use their hands much. My interpretation of the clutch has a strap. Gauge is important for this project; if your bag is too narrow or too wide it won't fit the hex frame properly.

Making the Bag

FINISHED MEASUREMENTS

Height of Bag: 6"/15cm, excluding strap

Width of Bag: 10 (12)"/25 (30)cm

To fit 10 (12)"/25 (30)cm wide hex-open frame. Directions are for the smaller size with the larger size in parentheses. If there is only one number, it applies to both sizes.

MATERIALS AND TOOLS

234 (312)yd/213 (284)m of **5** bulky weight novelty yarn, nylon/cotton/acrylic blend, in mauve

Knitting needles: 4.5 mm (size 7 U.S.), preferably metal, or size to obtain gauge

Straight hex-open frame, 10 (12)"/25 (30)cm wide

Pins

Blunt tapestry needle for sewing

Small amount of non-novelty yarn in matching color for sewing (optional)

2 silver snapper rings, ¼"/6mm

2 small silver key rings

Silver chain, approx 20"/51cm (or desired length)

Brooch

GAUGE

16 sts and 28 rows = 4"/10cm in Garter Stitch (knit every row), yarn doubled

Always take time to check your gauge.

Knitting

Hold two strands together throughout.
Cast on 40 (48) sts. Leave long tail for sewing.
Work in Garter Stitch for 105 rows.
Bind off. Leave long tail for sewing.

Finishing

With the wrong side of the knitted fabric facing up, fold approx 1"/2.5cm of knitted fabric over one side of the hex frame. Make sure the flat side of the frame is facing down and away from you. Pin in place. Using project yarn and tapestry needle, sew edge securely. For smoother sewing you can also use a non-novelty yarn in a matching color. Repeat for the other side. Weave in ends.

Fold the bag in half making sure the right sides are together. Pin the side seams in place. Using the tapestry needle and preferred yarn, sew edges securely. Weave in ends.

Turn the bag right side out. Assemble the hex frame using snapper rings instead of the pins included with the frame. To do this, squeeze the hex frame sides together, aligning the openings, and insert a snapper ring in one hole, making sure the ring faces up. Repeat on the other side. Sew a few stitches on each side to hide the hex frame. Weave in ends.

Attach key rings to both edges of strap chain. Attach key rings to snapper rings. Pin brooch on bag.

This Clutch was knit with:

3 (4) balls of Moda Dea's Curious, bulky weight, 45% nylon/28% cotton/27% acrylic, 1.76oz/50g = approx 78yd/71m per ball, color #9547

Feedback

Smaller size wooden needles can break when knitting a tight, thick fabric. Try using metal needles and bang your head.

Clutch REMIX

Keyring hardware makes it simple to swap out the strap for a different look.

Try a twine strap with oversized resin beads on each end.

Fuzz

It can't get any easier! Using big needles and doubled mohair, knit a rectangle and sew up the sides. Now's the time to get that I-cord maker going or scan the Remix for inspiration to create a bag that's unique.

33

Making the Bag

FINISHED MEASUREMENTS (AFTER FELTING)

Height of Bag: 6½"/17cm, excluding strap

Width of Bag: 9"/23cm

MATERIALS AND TOOLS

Color A: 180yd/164m of (**4**) medium weight yarn, feltable mohair/wool/nylon blend, in aqua

Color B: 33yd/30m of (**3**) light-weight yarn, wool or wool blend, in tweed

Knitting needles: 6.5 mm (size 10 ½ U.S.)

Double-pointed needles or circular needle, 3.5 mm (size 4 U.S.) or an I-cord maker

Pins

Sharp tapestry needle for sewing

2 large burnt-orange beads with large holes, 1"/3cm wide (for anchor beads)

Sew-on snap closure

GAUGE

Exact gauge is not essential for this project

Feedback

Gently brush the mohair to raise the nap and encourage loft.

Knitting

Hold two strands of A together throughout.

Using straight needles, cast on 30 sts. Leave long tail for sewing.

Work in Stockinette Stitch for 66 rows.

Bind off. Leave long tail for sewing.

Making the Straps

(Make 3)

Using double-pointed needles, circular needle, or I-cord maker, and B, make three 4 st I-cords, approx 21"/53cm long, following the instructions on page 18. Leave long tails on both ends to thread through anchor beads and to sew to the bag sides.

Finishing

Fold piece in half, bringing the cast-on edge up to meet the bind-off edge. With the right sides together, pin the side edges in place. Using the sharp tapestry needle and long tails, sew the side seams. Weave in ends.

Turn the bag right side out and follow the directions in the felting section to felt the bag.

Block the bag, if desired, using a book or grocery bags to shape. Check and adjust the shape to your liking. Allow the bag to dry.

Knot the tails of the three I-cords together. Thread the tails, at one end, through an anchor bead. Sew the tails to the inside side seam of the bag. Repeat this process on the other side. Weave in ends.

Sew on snap closure.

This Fuzz bag was knit with:

Classic Elite La Gran Mohair, medium weight, 76 1/2% mohair/17 1/2% wool/6% nylon, 1.5 oz/42g = approx 90yd/82m per ball

(A) 2 balls, color #6546

Tahki Yarns' Shannon, lightweight, 100% wool, 1.75oz/50g = approx 92yd/85m per ball

(B) 1 ball, color #16

FUZZ

REMIX

Napkin rings, beads, stripes, electrical cord, brooches, guitar strings, more beads, and purchased handles can all be used to create straps and embellish your bag.

Telephon

**The unique strap
used in this bag guarantees you'll always get a call
back. Although I offer two civilized ways to poke
holes in the cord, I just jammed a sharp-ended
tapestry needle through, and that worked just fine.**

FINISHED MEASUREMENTS

Height of Bag: 11"/28cm, excluding strap

Width of Bag: 10"/25cm

MATERIALS AND TOOLS

165yd/150m of (**6**) bulky weight yarn, wool/acrylic/nylon blend, in multi-colored pastels

Knitting needles: 6.5 mm (size 10.5 U.S.) and size 9 mm (size 13 U.S.)

Pins

5.5mm (size I-9 U.S.) crochet hook

Telephone cord, microphone cord, or other curly cable, at least 30"/76cm

Hammer and nail, or power hand drill and 1/16"/1.5mm size drill bit to drill holes in telephone cord

Short piece of board to drill or hammer on

Sharp tapestry needle

10 pieces of contrasting scrap yarn, each 20"/51cm

10 pieces of 17 pound test (or higher) clear fishing line, each 20"/51cm

Sew-on snap closure (optional)

GAUGE

Exact gauge is not essential for this project

Knitting

Using 6.5 mm (size 10.5 U.S.) needles, hold two strands together and cast on 24 sts loosely.

Work in Reverse Stockinette Stitch for 38 rows.

Change to 9 mm (size 13 U.S.) needles and four strands held together.

Work in Garter Stitch (knit every row) for 5 rows.

Change back to 6.5 mm (size 10.5 U.S.) needles and two strands held together.

Work in Reverse Stockinette Stitch for 44 rows.

Bind off loosely.

Assembling

Fold bag in half, with purl sides (right sides) together, bringing the cast-on edge up to meet the bind-off edge. Pin side edges together. Using the crochet hook and holding two strands of yarn together, join yarn with a slip stitch in side of bag. Single crochet (page 20) side edges together. Repeat to join other side.

Preparing the Strap

Using scissors, trim cord to the desired length. Make five holes in each cord end approx 1½"/4cm apart using a power hand drill, hammer and nail, or sharp tapestry needle.

Finishing

Using the sharp tapestry needle and contrasting scrap yarn, tack both sides of the strap to the inside seams of the bag. There should be five tack spots on each inside seam. Once both sides are tacked into place, swap out each piece of scrap yarn with a length of clear fishing line. Secure tightly and weave in ends.

Sew snap closure to the top center of bag sides.

This Telephone bag was knit with:

5 skeins of Katia's Diva, bulky weight, 63% wool/21% acrylic/16% nylon, 1.75oz/50g = approx 33yd/30m per skein, color #6101

Telephone

REMIX

When you play music you spend a lot of time around cords. Check out your local electronics surplus store or liquidation outlet for a variety of cables.

Feedback

Electric cords and cables are a great resource for purse straps. The crazy colors and shapes add instant design impact and structure to any bag.

Free Bird

RIFF

Finally, the perfect project to use those big, beautiful beads you've been collecting. Bright color is the element that ties these mismatched ones together. The large beads are easily sewn to the bag *after* felting. Otherwise, they'd be lost in the fluffiness of the mohair.

Making the Bag

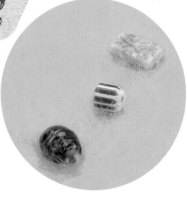

FINISHED MEASUREMENTS (AFTER FELTING)

Height of Bag: 18½"/47cm, excluding strap

Width of Bag: 11"/28cm

MATERIALS AND TOOLS

436yd/400m of (**4**) medium weight yarn, felt-able mohair/wool/nylon blend, in yellow

Knitting needles: 6 mm (size 10 U.S.) and 6.5 mm (size 10.5 U.S.)

Double-pointed needles or circular needle, 6.5 mm (size 10.5 U.S.)

Pins

Sharp tapestry needle for sewing

20 large blue or green beads with large hole, ½-¾"/1–2cm diameter

Dental floss threader, or needle with an eye large enough to thread mohair yarn but small enough to fit through the beads

Sew-on snap closure

GAUGE

Exact gauge is not essential for this project.

Knitting

Hold two strands together throughout.

Using 6 mm (size 10 U.S.) needles, cast on 40 sts. Leave a long tail for sewing.

Work in Stockinette Stitch for 4 rows.

Change to 6.5 mm (size 10.5 U.S.) needles.

Work in Stockinette Stitch for 104 rows.

Change to size 10 needles.

Work in Stockinette Stitch for 4 rows.

Bind off. Leave a long tail for sewing.

Making the Straps

(Make 2)
Using 6.5 mm (size 10.5 U.S.) double-pointed or circular needles, knit a 6 st I-cord following the instructions on page 18. I-cords should measure approx 28"/71cm or approx 100 rows each. Weave in ends.

Finishing

Fold bag in half, bringing the cast-on edge up to meet the bind-off edge. With right sides together, pin side edges together. Using sharp tapestry needle and long tails, sew side seams. Weave in ends.

Follow the felting instructions on page 16 to felt the bag and straps.

Slip book into bag to block, and allow all pieces to dry thoroughly.

Using approx 10"/25cm lengths of yarn and tapestry needle, sew 20 beads around the bottom of the bag. The beads should be placed about 2"/5cm up from the bottom edge and be spaced evenly apart. I have nine beads on the front, nine on the back, and one on each side, totaling 20 beads. Weave in ends.

Pin and sew straps to the outside of the bag. The bottom edge of each strap starts approx 5"/13cm up from the bottom of the bag, and the outer edges are approx 2½"/6cm in from each side. Weave in ends.

Sew snap closures to upper inside edges of bag at center.

This Free Bird bag was knit with:

4 balls Sunbeam Paris Mohair, medium weight, 81% mohair/11% wool/8% nylon, 1.75oz/50g = approx 109yd/100m per ball, color #1162

Feedback

Use a dental floss threader instead of a needle to thread yarn easily through beads.

REMIX

*Here I used blue
straps sewn on the
inside of the bag.*

Laura Petrie

RIFF This bag is knit in strips of color blocks. The simple graphic and unexpected color palette has a retro-futuristic look, but the possible color variations are endless. When the strips are sewn together, the seams provide extra support and structure. Working in strips is much easier than intarsia and is more convenient when traveling.

FINISHED MEASUREMENTS (AFTER FELTING)

Height of Bag: 8"/20cm, excluding strap

Width of Bag: 10"/25cm

MATERIALS AND TOOLS

Color A: 173yd/158m of 4 worsted weight yarn, wool, in purple

Color B: 173yd/158m of 4 worsted weight yarn, wool, in lilac

Color C: 173yd/158m of 4 worsted weight yarn, wool, in cordovan

Knitting needles: 4.5 mm (size 7 U.S.) and 3.75 mm (size 5 U.S.)

Sharp tapestry needle for sewing

2 cordovan leather straps with sew-on tabs, 27"/69cm

4 silver purse feet

Sew-on magnetic snap

GAUGE

Exact gauge is not essential for this project.

Basements and bars...rehearsing in Kim's basement for the Mountain Battles tour

Notes:

1. You'll start and end some strips with 4 rows worked on smaller needles. This will tighten up the bag opening and help prevent splaying when felting.

2. Leave approx 12"/30cm tails when changing colors. You will use these ends to sew corresponding blocks when assembling the bag.

Knitting

Long Strip

(Make 2)

Using smaller needles and A, cast on 18 sts.

Work in Garter Stitch (knit every row) for 4 rows.

Change to larger needles.

Work in Garter Stitch for 28 rows (total 32 rows with A).

With C, work in Garter Stitch for 32 rows.

With B, work in Garter Stitch for 32 rows.

With A, work in Garter Stitch for 32 rows.

With B, work in Garter Stitch for 32 rows.

With C, work in Garter Stitch for 32 rows.

With A, work in Garter Stitch for 28 rows.

Change to smaller needles.

With A, work in Garter Stitch for 4 rows.

Bind off.

Side Strip

(Make 2)

Using smaller needles and C, cast on 18 sts.

Work in Garter Stitch for 4 rows.

Change to larger needles.

Work in Garter Stitch for 28 rows (total 32 rows with C).

With B, work in Garter Stitch for 32 rows.

With A, work in Garter Stitch for 32 rows.

Bind off.

Center Strip

(Make 1)

Note: The last block of this strip is only 16 rows long (for front closure).

Using smaller needles and C, cast on 18 sts.

Work in Garter Stitch for 4 rows.

Change to larger needles.

Work in Garter Stitch for 28 rows (total 32 rows with C).

With B, work in Garter Stitch for 32 rows.

With A, work in Garter Stitch for 32 rows.

With C, work in Garter Stitch for 32 rows.

With A, work in Garter Stitch for 32 rows.

With B, work in Garter Stitch for 32 rows.

With C, work in Garter Stitch for 16 rows.

Bind off.

Tab

(Make 1)

Using larger needles and C, cast on 18 sts.

Work in Garter Stitch for 32 rows.

Bind off.

(Continues on next page)

What's in the Bag?

Flying

Tickets
Money
Passport
Earplugs
Water
Book
Chocolate

(Continued from previous page)

Assembling

With wrong sides facing up, arrange the strips as shown in figure 1.

Using the sharp tapestry needle and yarn tails, sew long strips to each side of center strip. The last block of the center strip will only extend halfway up the last block of the long strips. Take care to use a yarn tail that matches one of the blocks. It may be helpful to knot the tails together at each color change before sewing.

Sew one edge of the tab to the inside of the first color block of the center strip approx 1½"/4cm down from bag opening (approx between rows 12 and 13).

Sew one edge of each side strip to the edge of the central block of each long strip. Fold the bag like a box with no top, so that all the long edges of the side strips meet the edges of the long strips, and stitch up all four seams. Sew an extra stitch or two at each corner of the bag opening, to narrow the opening and reduce the tendency to splay during felting.

Finishing

Weave in the ends.

Turn the bag right side out. Follow the felting instructions on page 16 to felt the bag.

Block the bag by inserting a snug fitting book (I used a telephone directory) and allow it to dry.

Using the sharp tapestry needle and C, sew leather straps on right sides of front and back, centered in top block of long strips.

Attach the purse feet.

Attach the sew-on magnetic snap to underside of tab and right side of top block of center strip.

Figure 1

A—Purple

B—Lilac

C—Cordovan

- - - Broken lines indicate where sewing will take place

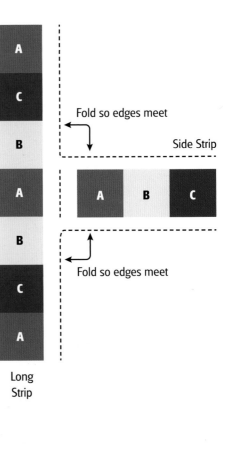

This Laura Petrie bag was knit with:

Brown Sheep Company's Nature Spun, worsted weight, 100% wool, 3.5oz/100g = approx 245yd/224m per skein

(A) 1 skein, color #N59

(B) 1 skein, color #N64

(C) 1 skein, color #N89

REMIX

Choose your own colors. Just remember that light and dark colors felt to different sizes. Swatch up a small test strip first.

Feedback

It's easier for me to line up the color blocks and sew the seams correctly if I knot the tail with its neighbor first.

The Tube

RIFF This bag gets its support from a tightly knit fabric and metal hoops sewn inside after the bag is assembled. Purse feet help define and stabilize the bottom. The strap is six strands of beaded fishing line—even people who can't bead (like me) can make it!

FINISHED MEASUREMENTS

Height of Bag: 4½"/11cm, excluding strap

Width of Bag: 7"/18cm

MATERIALS AND TOOLS

308yd/284m of (4) worsted or 3 DK weight yarn, cotton, in blue/white

Knitting needles: 4.5 mm (size 7 U.S.), preferably metal, or size to obtain gauge

6 lengths of 17# test fishing line, 24"/61cm long

1 large package white pearl beads, 4mm

2 white pearl beads, approx 15mm, for anchor beads

Blunt tapestry needle for sewing

Pins

2 metal hoops, 4"/10cm diameter

Sew-on magnetic snap

4 silver purse feet

GAUGE

17 sts and 32 rows = 4"/10cm in Garter Stitch (knit every row), yarn doubled

Always take time to check your gauge.

Knitting

Bag Side

(Make 2)
Hold two strands together throughout.
Cast on 5 sts. Leave long tails for sewing.
Row 1: Kfb, k3, kfb (7 sts).
Row 2: Kfb, k5, kfb (9 sts).
Row 3: Kfb, k7, kfb (11 sts).
Row 4: Kfb, k9, kfb (13 sts).
Row 5: Kfb, k11, kfb (15 sts).
Row 6: Knit.
Row 7: Kfb, k13, kfb (17 sts).
Rows 8 – 10: Knit.
Row 11: Kfb, k15, kfb (19 sts).
Rows 12 – 18: Knit.
Row 19: K2tog, k15, k2tog (17 sts).
Rows 20 – 22: Knit.
Row 23: K2tog, k13, k2tog (15 sts).
Row 24: Knit.
Row 25: K2tog, k11, k2tog (13 sts).
Row 26: K2tog, k9, k2tog (11 sts).
Row 27: K2tog, k7, k2tog (9 sts).
Row 28: K2tog, k5, k2tog (7 sts).
Row 29: K2tog, k3, k2tog (5 sts).
Bind off. Leave long tails for sewing.

Bag Body

Hold two strands together throughout.
Cast on 28 sts. Leave long tails for sewing seams.
Rows 1 – 98: Knit.
Bind off. Leave long tails for sewing.

Feedback

Use sturdy binder clips to secure the unknotted ends of beaded strands while you're working with them.

Bag Flap

Hold two strands together throughout.
Cast on 26 sts. Leave long tail for sewing.
Rows 1 – 23: Knit.
Row 24: K2tog, k22, k2tog (24 sts).
Row 25: K2tog, k20, k2tog (22 sts).
Row 26: K2tog, k18, k2tog (20 sts).
Row 27: K2tog, k16, k2tog (18 sts).
Row 28: K2tog, k14, k2tog (16 sts).
Row 29: Knit.
Row 30: K2tog, k12, k2tog (14 sts).
Row 31: K2tog, k10, k2tog (12 sts).
Row 32: K2tog, k8, k2tog (10 sts).
Row 33: K2tog, k6, k2tog (8 sts).
Row 34: K2tog, k4, k2tog (6 sts).
Row 35: K2tog, k2, k2tog (4 sts).
Bind off. Weave in end.

Making the Strap

Bead six strands of fishing line. Beaded lengths should be approx 14½"/37cm. Thread large anchor bead on one end of strap, over all six strands, and knot ends together. Leave long tails to sew the strap to the bag. Repeat on other end of strap.

Finishing

Using the blunt tapestry needle and one strand of yarn, sew the cast-on edge of the flap to the bag between rows 10 and 11. The side with the flap sewn onto it will now be the right side of the bag.

With the right side out, roll the bag body into a cylinder. Where the edges meet, sew ½"/1cm in from both outside edges. This will create the bag opening.

Pin a side circle to a side opening and sew along the edge. Repeat for the other side.

Position a metal hoop against the side circle inside the bag. Tack into place. Repeat for the other side.

Sew magnetic snap to bag flap and bag body.

Use the fishing line at the strap ends and sew the strap to the top of the bag. Hide ends.

Attach the purse feet.

The Tube bag was knit with:

2 skeins of Tahki's Cotton Dot, DK weight, 100% mercerized cotton, 3.5oz/100g = approx 154yd/142m per skein, color #510

The Tube REMIX

For knitting purists, try three lengths of I-cord.

Here's the same bag with a purchased beaded handle.

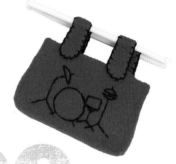

Moe

RIFF

This bag is for the John Bonham in us all. If you're not ~~supporting~~ dating a drummer, remember that purchased straight handles will work just as well as drumsticks.

Making the Bag

FINISHED MEASUREMENTS (AFTER FELTING)

Height of Bag: 7"/18cm, excluding strap

Width of Bag: 10½"/27cm

MATERIALS AND TOOLS

Color A: 250yd/229m of (5) chunky weight yarn, wool, in red

Color B: 17yd/16m of (5) chunky weight yarn, wool, in black

Knitting needles: 6 mm (size 10 U.S.)

Stitch markers

Pins

Sharp tapestry needle for sewing and embroidery

Washable marker in a dark color to trace design template

1 pair of drumsticks, junior size, approx 12½"/32cm long

GAUGE

Exact gauge is not essential for this project.

Knitting

Main Body Panel

With A, cast on 38 sts. Leave long tail for sewing.

Rows 1 – 16: Knit (38 sts).

Row 17: K1, kfb, k34, kfb, k1 (40 sts).

Rows 18 – 32: Knit.

Row 33: K1, kfb, k36, kfb, k1 (42 sts).

Rows 34 – 48: Knit.

Row 49: K1, kfb, k38, kfb, k1 (44 sts).

Rows 50 – 84: Knit.

Place a st marker at the beginning and end of Row 56 and Row 77. This denotes the bottom of the bag and will help to position the Side Panels when assembling the bag.

Row 85: K1, k2tog, k38, k2tog, k1 (42 sts).

Rows 86 – 100: Knit.

Row 101: K1, k2tog, k36, k2tog, k1 (40 sts).

Rows 102 – 116: Knit.

Row 117: K1, k2tog, k34, k2tog, k1 (38 sts).

Rows 118 – 132: Knit.

Bind off. Leave long tail for sewing.

Side Panel

(Make 2)

With A, cast on 6 sts. Leave long tail for sewing.

Rows 1 – 14: Knit.

Row 15: K1, kfb, k2, kfb, k1 (8 sts).

Rows 16 – 28: Knit.

Row 29: K1, kfb, k4, kfb, k1 (10 sts).

Rows 30 – 42: Knit.

Row 43: K1, kfb, k6, kfb, k1 (12 sts).

Rows 44 – 55: Knit.

Bind off. Leave long tail for sewing.

Strap Tabs

(Make 4)

With A, cast on 6 sts and work in Garter Stitch (knit every row) for 50 rows or approx 7"/18cm. Bind off. Weave in ends.

Assembling

Position the bind off edge of a side panel to the side of the main body panel, in between the stitch markers, and pin in place. Using A and sharp tapestry needle, sew in place.

Remove the stitch markers and pin side edges of the side panel in place, making sure that the top edge of the side panel and the top edges of the main body panel are even. Sew in place and weave in the ends.

Repeat for the other side of the bag.

Backstage somewhere, before some show, some time...

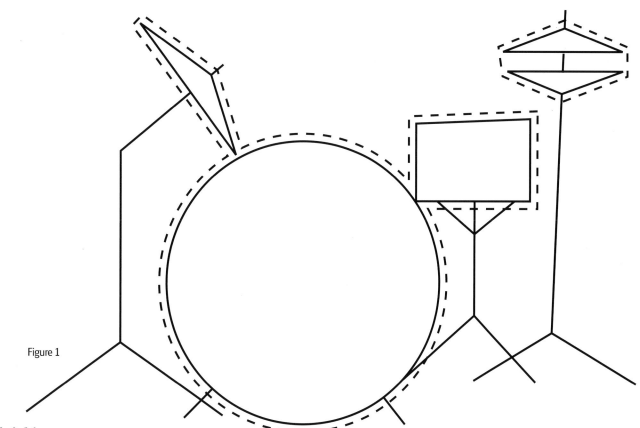

Figure 1

Finishing

Follow the felting instructions on page 16 to felt the bag and the four strap tabs.

Block the bag by inserting a snug fitting book. Tuck a couple plastic grocery bags down at the bottom of the bag on each side of the book to give the bottom more girth. Lay the strap tabs flat and place something flat and heavy (another book perhaps?) on them. Allow all the pieces to dry.

Using B and a sharp tapestry needle, follow the Moe Template (figure 1) and embroider the design. I recommend making a photocopy of the Moe Template and then cutting out the four larger

(Continues on next page)

What's in the Bag?

Backstage

Earplugs
Assortment of guitar
and bass picks
Passes/laminates
Bus key
Tour book
Set list
Knitting project

(Continued from previous page)

figures along the dotted lines. Start with the big circle (the kick drum) and pin it in place. Use the washable marker to draw around it. Unpin it, then, using the Back Stitch (page 21), embroider the shapes. Don't worry if you can see the marker. It comes out by gently rubbing the area with a damp towel. Embroider the remaining three larger pieces and the straight lines (the drum hardware). Weave in all ends.

Using the sharp tapestry needle and B, embroider Blanket Stitch (page 21) around the four strap tabs. Weave in the ends.

Using the sharp tapestry needle and A, fold the strap tab evenly over a drumstick and sew four or five small sts right under the drumstick. You are creating a snug pocket to hold the stick in place. Repeat this process for each tab.

Position and sew the bottom of the strap tab to the right side of the bag. Repeat for all tabs. Turn the bag inside out and sew the bottom of the other side of the strap tab to the wrong side of the bag. Repeat this process for all tabs. It can help to have the drumstick inserted while positioning the tabs. Just remove it if sewing becomes awkward. Weave in ends.

Insert the drumsticks.

This Moe bag was knit with:

Naturally's Alpine Chunky, chunky weight, 100% wool, 7oz/200g = approx 240yd/220m per hank

(A) 1 hank, color #3003

(B) 1 hank, color #3010

Feedback

After embroidering and attaching the straps to the bag, it started to look less crisp, so I re-blocked it by reinserting the blocking materials, misting it with water, and then pressing it with a steam iron on the wool setting. This method works with any felted bag that's losing its shape or just needs freshening up.

Moe

REMIX

Any two sturdy sticks can be handles for this bag. These are purchased straight handles that I spray-painted black.

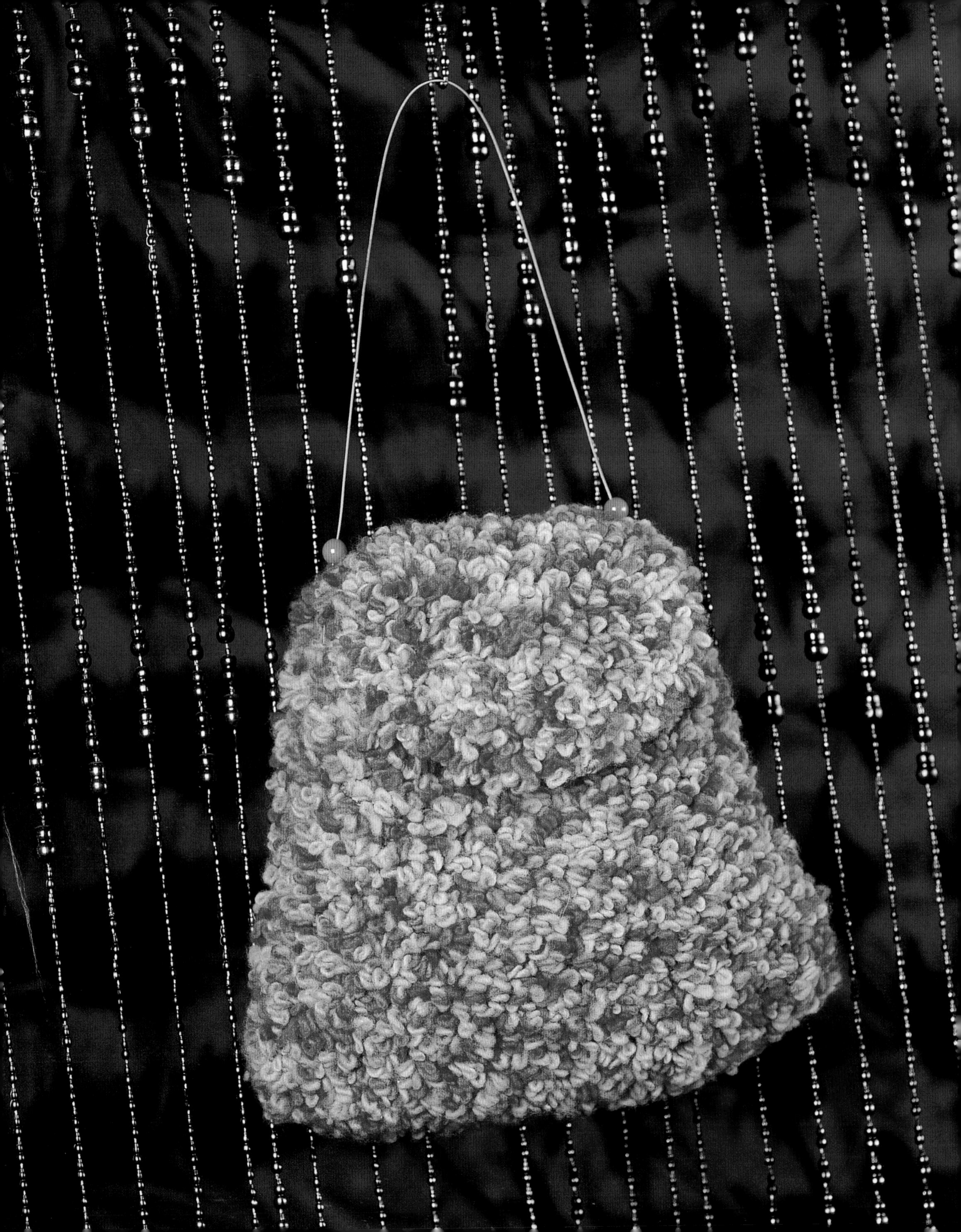

Loopy

RIFF

Loopy, like your best friend! Super bulky yarn and big needles make this simple bag a quick knit in Reverse Stockinette Stitch. The purl side is the right side. The bag looks great without a flap, too—check the Remix to see.

Making the Bag

FINISHED MEASUREMENTS

Height of Bag: 9"/23cm, excluding strap

Width of Bag: 11"/28cm, at widest point

MATERIALS AND TOOLS

192yd/176m of **6** super bulky yarn, wool/nylon blend, pink and orange pallette

Knitting needles: 9 mm (size 13 U.S.) and 10 mm (size 15 U.S.)

Pins

6mm (size J-10 U.S.) crochet hook

Blunt tapestry needle for sewing

Wire cutters or scissors

Acoustic guitar string, medium gauge, bronze wound, low E

4 copper splice caps or large crimps

Pliers or crimpers

2 small copper or gold crimps

2 hot pink beads, 2/5"/1cm

Gold colored bead wire, 34 gauge

Sew-on magnetic snap

GAUGE

Exact gauge is not essential for this project.

Knitting

Hold two strands together.
Using smaller needles, cast on 18 sts.
Beginning with a purl row (RS), work in Reverse Stockinette Stitch for 23 rows.
Change to larger needles and hold four strands together.
Row 24: Knit.
Row 25: BO 1 st, p16, BO 1 st (16 sts).
Row 26: Knit.
Row 27: P1, m1, p14, m1, p1 (18 sts).
Row 28: Knit.
Change to smaller needles and hold two strands together.
Work in Reverse Stockinette Stitch for 23 rows.
Bind off.

Making the Flap

Hold two strands together throughout.
Using smaller needles, cast on 14 sts.
Work in Stockinette Stitch for 6 rows.
Row 7: K2tog tbl, k10, k2tog tbl (12 sts).
Work in Stockinette Stitch for 11 rows.
Row 19: *K2tog tbl, k2; repeat from * to end (9 sts).
Row 20: *P2tog, p1; repeat from * to end (6 sts).
Row 21: K2tog tbl, k2, k2tog tbl (4 sts).
Bind off purlwise. Weave in ends.

Assembling

Fold bag in half, bringing the cast-on edge up to meet the bind-off edge. With right sides (purl sides) together, pin side edges of bag together. Using the crochet hook and holding two strands of yarn together, join yarn with a slip stitch in a side of the bag and single crochet (page 20) the side of the bag together. Repeat to join other side of bag. Weave in ends. **Tip:** Use crochet hook to weave in ends.

With the right sides (purl sides) of the bag and flap together, position and pin the edge of the flap to the opening edge of the bag. Using the blunt tapestry needle and one strand of yarn, sew the flap edge to the bag edge. Weave in ends.

Preparing the Strap

Using wire cutters or scissors, trim the ends of the guitar string. You will be working with just the wire.

Fold the end of the wire 2½–3"/6–8cm from the end, creating a loop. Pinch the loop in place. Slip the loop through the splice cap or large crimp to the end of the looped wire and using pliers or crimper, crimp to secure in place. Position and crimp a second crimp on the loop halfway between the end of the loop and the first crimp. See page 15 for photograph of assembly. Do not repeat this for the other end yet.

Now you need to load up the wire as follows. Thread one crimp right side up, one bead right side up (if there is a right side), one bead upside down, and one crimp upside down. The beads will be positioned after the strap is attached to the bag. Repeat on the other end of the wire.

Finishing

Using the gold colored bead wire and tapestry needle, sew the strap edges to the outsides of the bag. Position the bottom of the loop of each strap end approx 4"/10cm down from the top of the side seam. Weave in ends.

Using pliers or crimpers, position crimps approx 1"/3cm from the top of the bag. Slide the bead into place.

Sew snap to wrong side of flap and right side of bag.

This Loopy bag was knit with:

5 balls of GGH Tibet, super bulky weight, 91% wool/9% nylon, 1.75 oz/50g = approx 47yd/43m per ball, color #3

Feedback

To prevent pens, pencils, and other sharp items from poking through the sides of the bag, sew a little pouch. Cut a 10 x 8-inch (25 x 20cm) rectangle out of any fabric, fold, sew up the sides, and hem the open edges. Sew on a snap closure to keep things in place.

Loopy

REMIX

Here it is without a flap. Don't have a guitar string handy? Try a triple I-cord with beads.

Road

RIFF

This bag, in maroon, is what I carry. It sits perfectly under the airplane seat in front of me. If you've been reluctant to knit using double-pointed needles, this is the perfect project. It knits up fast with big yarn and big needles.

FINISHED MEASUREMENTS (AFTER FELTING)

Height of Bag: 7½"/19cm, excluding strap and tabs

Width of Bag: 11"/28cm, at widest point

MATERIALS AND TOOLS

275yd/250m of ⑥ bulky weight yarn, wool, in blue

Knitting needles: 10 mm (size 15 U.S.) double-pointed needles, and 10 mm (size 15 U.S.) circular needles, 16"/40cm long

Stitch markers

Stitch holder

Blunt tapestry needle

2 silver metal rings, 1½"/38mm

Approx 30"/76cm of inseam cut from a jean leg

Approx 4yd/4m of blue heavy duty cotton yarn

Silver sew-on or pronged magnetic snap

Assorted patches and pins (optional)

GAUGE

Exact gauge is not essential for this project.

Making the Bag

Knitting

Bag Bottom/Body

Using double-pointed needles, cast on 6 sts. Distribute the sts over 3 needles, placing 2 sts on each needle. Join to work in rounds, being careful not to twist stitches. Place stitch marker to denote beginning of round.

Round 1: Knit.
Round 2: Kfb in each st (12 sts).
Round 3: Knit.
Round 4: Kfb in each st (24 sts).
Round 5: Knit.
Round 6: *K1, kfb in next st; repeat from * around (36 sts).
Round 7: Knit.
Round 8: *K2, kfb in next st; repeat from * around (48 sts).
Note: You may wish to start using a fourth dpn, to accommodate all of the stitches.
Round 9: Knit.
Round 10: *K3, kfb in next st; repeat from * around (60 sts).
Note: You may wish to change to a circular needle here.
Round 11: Knit.

Round 12: *K4, kfb in next st; repeat from * around (72 sts).
Round 13: Knit.
Round 14: *K5, kfb in next st; repeat from * around (84 sts).
Rounds 15 – 35: Knit.
Place a marker on round 28 for pocket placement.
Round 36: K19, k2tog, k19, ssk, k19, k2tog, k19, ssk (80 sts).
Round 37: Knit.
Round 38: K18, k2tog, k18, ssk, k18, k2tog, k18, ssk (76 sts).
Round 39: Knit.
Round 40: K17, k2tog, k17, ssk, k17, k2tog, k17, ssk (72 sts).
Round 41: Knit.
Round 42: K16, k2tog, k16, ssk, k16, k2tog, k16, ssk (68 sts).
Round 43: Knit.
Round 44: K15, k2tog, k15, ssk, k15, k2tog, k15, ssk (64 sts).
Rounds 45 – 52: Knit.

Shaping Front Opening

Set-up: K4, place next 6 sts on st holder (for beginning of front opening), turn work.

Note: Work back and forth in rows. Turn at the end of each row.

Row 53: P2tog, p2tog, p54 (56 sts).

Row 54: Ssk, ssk, k48, k2tog, k2tog (52 sts).

Row 55: P2tog, p2tog, p44, p2tog tbl, p2tog tbl (48 sts).

Row 56: Ssk, ssk, k42, k2tog (45 sts).

Row 57: P43, p2tog tbl (44 sts).

Bind off Sides and Shape Flap

Row 58: K11 (side of bag), k22 (flap), BO 11 sts (other side of bag), cut yarn (33 sts).

Row 59: Reattach yarn knitwise in first st of other side, BO 11 sts (side of bag), k22 (flap) (22 sts).

Beginning with a purl row, work in Stockinette Stitch (knit on RS, purl on WS) for 16 rows.

Row 76: P2tog, p18, p2tog tbl (20 sts).

Row 77: Knit.

Row 78: P2tog, p16, p2tog tbl (18 sts).

Row 79: Knit.

Row 80: P2tog, p14, p2tog tbl (16 sts).

Row 81: Knit.

Row 82: P2tog, p12, p2tog tbl (14 sts).

Row 83: Knit.

Row 84: P2tog, p10, p2tog tbl (12 sts).

Row 85: Ssk, k8, k2tog (10 sts).

Row 86: P2tog, p6, p2tog tbl (8 sts).

Row 87: Ssk, k4, k2tog (6 sts).

Row 88: P2tog, p2, p2tog tbl (4 sts).

Bind off.

(Continues on next page)

(Continued from previous page)

Finishing Front Opening

Bind off the 6 sts on stitch holder at beginning of front opening.

Making the Strap Tabs

Row 1: Pick up and knit 6 sts from bag side leaving 1 st between flap edge and tab edge.
Work in Garter Stitch (knit every row) for 11 rows.
Bind off. Repeat on other side.

Making the Back Pocket

Pick up and knit 16 sts along row 28 (marked row) at the center of the back of the bag.
Work in Stockinette Stitch for 20 rows.
Bind off. Using the blunt tapestry needle, sew the sides of the pocket to the bag.

Finishing

Slip silver ring onto strap tab, fold, and using blunt tapestry needle, sew tab edge to the inside of the bag. Repeat on the other side.

Weave in all ends.

Using a steam iron on wool setting, press flap gently.

Follow the felting instructions on page 16 to felt the bag.

While still damp, use an iron on wool setting to press the flap flat. Use plastic bags to block bag. Don't overstuff it. Allow the bag to dry.

Cut the inseam out of one leg of an old pair of jeans, approx 30"/76cm long. Fold approx 2"/5cm of one end of the inseam around a strap ring.

With heavy duty cotton yarn, use an Albright Special knot to attach the jean inseam to the strap hoops.

To make this knot, insert the cotton through the loop that is formed by the jean inseam. Pull 10–12"/25–30cm of yarn through to give yourself ample yarn to work with (figure 1).

Now wrap the yarn back over itself, and over the doubled inseam while gripping the yarn and the inseam loop together with your thumb and finger. Continue winding the yarn around until you reach the edge with the silver ring on it. Insert the

end of the yarn back through the inseam loop once more at the point of the original entry (figure 2). Before releasing your thumb-and-finger grip, pull gently on each yarn end to remove slack. Pull on long end of inseam to close loop around the silver ring.

For the last stage of tightening, pull on both ends of yarn and on the jean inseam (figure 3). Secure the yarn ends with an overhand knot. Weave in and trim ends. Repeat on the other end.

Attach either a sew-on magnetic snap, or a pronged magnetic snap, to wrong side of flap and right side of front of bag.

(Optional): Attach patches and pins as desired.

This Road bag was knit with:

5 skeins of Hawthorne Cottage Yarns' Chunky Wool, bulky weight, 100% wool, 3.5oz/100g = approx 55yd/50m per skein, #36 The Blues

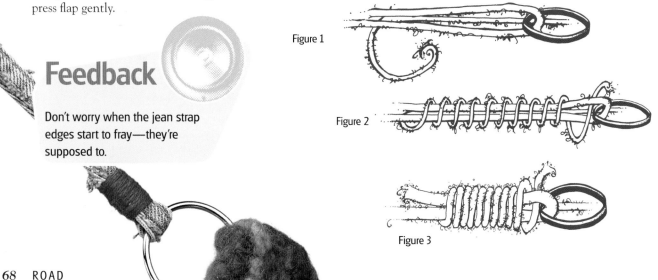

Feedback

Don't worry when the jean strap edges start to fray—they're supposed to.

Figure 1

Figure 2

Figure 3

Road

REMIX

Not a road dog?
Make it without the
patches and pins.

Edie

RIFF

I don't wear scarves, but I remember my mother wearing them. The strange color combinations and "mod" graphics found in vintage scarves make them little pieces of art. Don't hide them in the back of the closet!

Making the Bag

FINISHED MEASUREMENTS (AFTER FELTING)

Height of Bag: 6½"/17cm, excluding strap

Width of Bag: 9"/23cm

MATERIALS AND TOOLS

110yd/101m of ⑤ chunky Icelandic or Lopi yarn, wool, in rust

Knitting needles: 6.5 mm (size 10.5 U.S.)

Scarf, approx 24 x 24"/61 x 61cm

Needle and thread to match scarf to tack in shape (if needed)

Pins

Sharp tapestry needle

2 large gold eyelets, ¼"/6mm

Eyelet setter tool to fit ¼"/6mm eyelet

Hammer

Sew-on snap closure

GAUGE

Exact gauge is not essential for this project.

Knitting

Cast on 36 sts. Leave a long tail for sewing.

Work in Stockinette Stitch (knit on RS, purl on WS) for 70 rows.

Bind off. Leave a long tail for sewing.

Preparing the Strap

Press the scarf according to fabric requirements. With the wrong side up and placed as a diamond, fold the left and right corners towards the center, overlapping the points. Fold the outermost side edges again towards the center, overlapping them. Press and, if desired, tack into place.

Finishing

With the right sides together, pin the side edges together. Using the sharp tapestry needle and the long tails, sew the side seams. Take an extra stitch or two on the top edge of the bag on each side. This will narrow the bag opening and allow extra support for the eyelet. Weave in ends.

Follow the felting instructions on page 16 to felt the bag.

Stuff the bag with plastic bags to block. Allow it to dry.

Affix an eyelet at the top of both side seams near the bag opening. Work on a firm, protected surface and mark the position of the eyelet with a pen. Use a small knitting needle to create an opening just large enough for the eyelet to get through. Insert the deep half of the eyelet through the hole, from the outside to the inside of the bag. Position the shallow half of the eyelet over the deep half from the inside of the bag. Place the wide end of the eyelet tool over the shallow half of the eyelet and strike firmly with a hammer so that the stem of the deep half rolls over the shallow half. Refer to the instructions that come with the eyelet tool.

Feedback

Thrift stores, flea markets, and swap meets are great places to shop for vintage scarves *and* guitar amps.

Slip a scarf end, from the outside to the inside of the bag, through the eyelet opening and tie a knot. Repeat for the other side.

Sew on the snap closure.

This Edie bag was knit with:

1 hank 2 ply, Alafoss Plötulopi, 100% wool, 3.85oz/110g = approx 361yd/330m, color #9988 orange rust

Here's the same vintage scarf on a bag knit using yarn in a coordinating color.

Edie

REMIX

Propeller

RIFF

The more garish the colors, the better this bag looks. It's a great accessory for the petrochemical generation. Embroider the motifs wherever you like, but don't forget to wrap a couple of propellers around the sides and the bottom of the bag.

Making the Bag

FINISHED MEASUREMENTS (AFTER FELTING)

Height of Bag: 7½"/19cm, excluding strap

Width of Bag: 10½"/27cm

MATERIALS AND TOOLS

Color A: 264yd/241m of (**4**) worsted weight yarn, wool, in red-orange

Color B: 88yd/80m of (**4**) worsted weight yarn, wool, in maroon

Knitting needles: 5mm (size 8 U.S.)

Blunt tapestry needle for embroidery

Sharp tapestry needle for sewing

1 large safety pin, size 3

1½yd/1.4m poly cord upholstery piping, ½"/13mm diameter

4 gold rings, 2½"/6cm wide

Sew-on snap closure

GAUGE

Exact gauge is not essential for this project.

Knitting

With A, cast on 50 sts.
Work in Stockinette Stitch
(knit on RS, purl on WS)
for 120 rows.
Bind off.

Assembling

Using a steam iron on wool setting, press the edges of the bag to prevent rolling. This will make it easier to work with.

Using the blunt tapestry needle and B, Duplicate Stitch (page 21) the Propeller Motif (figure 1), seven times. Place the motifs randomly around bag, allow some of the motifs to wrap around the sides and bottom of the bag. Weave in all ends.

Fold the bag in half, bringing the cast-on edge up to meet the bind-off edge. Using the sharp tapestry needle and matching color yarn, sew the sides of the bag together. Weave in all ends.

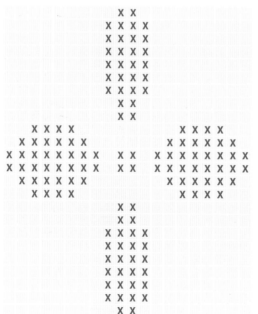

Figure 1

Making the Straps

(Make 2)
With A, cast on 13 sts. Leave a long tail for sewing.

Work in Stockinette Stitch for 120 rows.

Bind off. Leave a long tail for sewing

Assembling the Straps

Using long tails, sew edges together to form tubes. Weave in ends.

Finishing

Follow the felting instructions on page 16 to felt the bag and the straps.

Slip a book into the bag to block and allow it to dry.

Using the large safety pin, thread upholstery piping through felted tubes and allow them to dry.

Trim excess piping and sew ends of each tube closed. Weave in ends.

Using the sharp tapestry needle and matching yarn, sew the bottom half of each metal ring directly to the inside of the bag. Check the front of the bag often to ensure your work is not visible. Weave in ends.

Fold the end of one felted tube around a metal ring and sew. Repeat for other three tube ends and metal rings. Weave in ends.

Sew on snap closure.

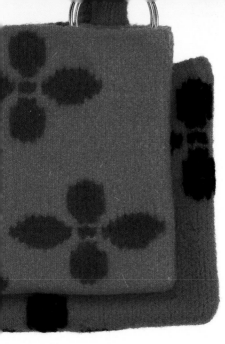

Propeller
REMIX

This Propeller bag was knit with:

Cascade Yarns' 220, worsted weight, 100% wool, 3.5oz/100g = approx 220yd/201m per skein.

(A) 2 skeins, color #7830

(B) 1 skein, color #8884

Feedback

To sew tubes easily, wrap the edges around a large knitting needle or drumstick. It's the same concept as using a darning egg to sew your socks.

Here it is in fuchsia with black propellers and metal hoops.

Heart

Don't let the length of this pattern fool you: This is an easy bag to knit. Mohair felts fast, so be careful! Set your machine for a light or normal wash. You can always re-felt a project smaller, but never bigger.

FINISHED MEASUREMENTS

Height of Bag (before felting):
18"/46cm, excluding strap

Width of Bag (before felting):
13½"/34cm

Height of Bag (after felting once):
14"/36cm, excluding strap

Width of Bag (after felting once):
13"/33cm

Height of Bag (after felting twice):
10½"/27cm, excluding strap

Width of Bag (after felting twice):
12"/30cm

Felting the heart twice makes the
bag smaller and denser. Check
these finished measurements
for approximate sizes.

MATERIALS AND TOOLS

300yd/274m of (4) worsted weight
yarn, felt-able mohair/wool/
nylon blend, in red

Knitting needles: 8 mm (size
11 U.S.)

Pins

Sharp tapestry needle for sewing

1½yd/1.4m satin cording, in silver
and black

Finer weight yarn in matching color
for sewing strap ends

Key

Sew-on snap closure

Row counter (recommended)

GAUGE

Exact gauge is not essential for
this project

Knitting

Side

(Make 2)
Hold two strands together
throughout.

Shaping Bottom of Bag

Beginning at bottom of bag, cast
   on 2 sts. Leave a long tail for
   sewing.
Row 1: Knit.
Row 2: Purl.
Row 3: Kfb twice (4 sts).
Row 4: Purl.
Row 5: K1, kfb twice, k1 (6 sts).
Row 6: Purl.
Row 7: Knit.
Row 8: P1, pfb, purl to last 2 sts,
   pfb, p1 (8 sts).
Row 9: Knit.
Rows 10 – 15: Repeat rows 8 and 9
   three times (14 sts).
Row 16: Purl.
Row 17: K1, kfb, knit to last 2 sts,
   kfb, k1 (16 sts).
Row 18: Purl.
Rows 19 – 24: Repeat rows 17 and
   18 three times (22 sts).
Row 25: Knit.
Row 26 – 33: Repeat rows 8 and 9
   four times (30 sts).
Row 34: Purl.
Rows 35 – 42: Repeat rows 17 and
   18 four times (38 sts).
Row 43: Knit.
Rows 44 – 47: Repeat rows 8 and 9
   twice (42 sts).
Row 48: Purl.
Row 49: Knit.
Row 50: Purl.
Rows 51 and 52: Repeat rows 17
   and 18 (44 sts).
Row 53: Knit.
Row 54: P2tog, p40, p2tog (42 sts).
Row 55: Knit.

Shaping Top Left Side

Row 56: P21, turn work to begin
   top left side shaping; leave
   remaining st unworked (21 sts).
Row 57: K2tog, k19 (20 sts).
Row 58: Purl.
Row 59: K18, k2tog (19 sts).
Row 60: P17, p2tog (18 sts).
Row 61: K16, k2tog (17 sts).
Row 62: P2tog, p13, p2tog (15 sts).
Row 63: K2tog, k11, k2tog (13 sts).
Row 64: P2tog, p9, p2tog (11 sts).
Row 65: K2tog, k7, k2tog (9 sts).
Row 66: P2tog, p2tog, p3, p2tog
   (6 sts).
Row 67: K2tog 3 times (3 sts).
Bind off. Leave a long tail for
   sewing.

Shaping Top Right Side

Join yarn purlwise in first unworked
    st following left side, to begin
    top right side shaping.
Row 56: P21 (21 sts).
Row 57: K19, k2tog (20 sts).
Row 58: Purl.
Row 59: K2tog, k18 (19 sts).
Row 60: P2tog, p17 (18 sts).
Row 61: K2tog, k16 (17 sts).
Row 62: P2tog, p13, p2tog (15 sts).
Row 63: K2tog, k11, k2tog (13 sts).
Row 64: P2tog, p9, p2tog (11 sts).
Row 65: K2tog, k7, k2tog (9 sts).
Row 66: P2tog, p3, p2tog, p2tog
    (6 sts).
Row 67: K2tog 3 times (3 sts).
Bind off. Leave a long tail for
    sewing.

Finishing

With right sides together, pin
outer edge from cast-on edge at
the bottom of the heart to bind-off
edges on the top of both sides of
the heart. Use long tails to sew side
seams. Weave in ends.

Turn bag right side out. Follow the
felting instructions on page 16 to
felt the bag. Check the progress of
the felting frequently; mohair felts
quickly.

Lay bag flat and allow it to dry.

Using the tapestry needle and
matching yarn, sew the ends of the
satin cording to the inside seams of
the bag opening. Sew the ends of
the cording along the entire length
of both bumps. This will help the
bag keep its heart shape. Use the
finer weight yarn in a matching
color if desired. Weave in ends.

Sew dangling key to point of heart.
Weave in ends.

Sew snap closure to the inside
edges of bag at center.

This Heart bag was knit with:

4 balls of Ironstone's English
Mohair, worsted weight, 78%
mohair/13% wool/9% nylon,
1.4oz/40g = approx 89yd/82m per
ball, color #403

What's in the Bag?

Touring

Earplugs
Book
Knitting project
Water
Passport
*Portable CD player
and headphones*

Feedback

A row counter takes the hassle out of keeping
track of rows while you work. Just remember to
register each row as you complete it.

Heart

REMIX

Make a Goth version with black mohair and a handcuff key ring. It says, "Give me your heart and I'll break it and stomp on the pieces."

Sari

Okay, so I went a little craft crazy. Touring got so boring that soaking branches in the hotel bathtub seemed like a good idea. The Remix offers a purchased wooden handle for you knitters who actually have a life.

Making the Bag

FINISHED MEASUREMENTS

Height of Bag: 6"/15cm, excluding strap

Width of Bag: 10½"/27cm

MATERIALS AND TOOLS

513yd/469m of (4) worsted weight yarn, 2nd grade recycled silk, in multi-colors

Knitting needles: 6 mm (size 10 U.S.), or size to obtain gauge

Blunt tapestry needle

Pins

Non-novelty yarn in coordinating color for sewing

(Optional) melamine, laminate, or stiff plastic oval to fit bottom of bag, approx 10 x 7"/25 x 18cm at widest point

Approx 6 grapevine branches, each 33"/84cm long

Fishing line, approx 4yd/4m

Polyurethane

Sponge brush to apply polyurethane

2"/5cm length of grapevine branch for twig closure

Hammer and nail or power hand drill and appropriate size drill bit to drill hole in twig closure

GAUGE

15 sts and 26 rows = 4"/10cm in established bag body stitch pattern, yarn doubled

Always take time to check your gauge.

Knitting

Bag Body

Hold two strands together throughout.

Cast on 27 sts. Leave a long tail for sewing.

Row 1: K1, *sl 1 wyif, move yarn to back and k1; rep from * to end.

Row 2 (RS): P2,*sl 1 wyib, move yarn to front and p1; rep from * to end.

Rows 3 – 178: Repeat Rows 1 and 2. Piece should measure approx 27"/69cm.

Bind off. Leave a long tail for sewing.

Bag Bottom

Hold two strands together throughout.

Cast on 8 sts.

Row 1 (RS): Knit.

Row 2: Pfb, p6, pfb (10 sts).

Row 3: Kfb, k8, kfb (12 sts).

Row 4: Pfb, p10, pfb (14 sts).

Row 5: Kfb, k12, kfb (16 sts).

Row 6: Pfb, p14, pfb (18 sts).

Row 7: Kfb, k16, kfb (20 sts).

Row 8: Purl.

Row 9: Kfb, k18, kfb (22 sts).

Row 10: Purl.

Row 11: Knit.

Row 12: Pfb, p20, pfb (24 sts).

Row 13: Knit.

Row 14: Purl.

Row 15: Kfb, k22, kfb (26 sts).

Work in Stockinette Stitch (knit on RS, purl on WS) for 14 rows.

Row 30: Bind off 1 st, p22, bind off 1 st (24 sts).

Row 31: Knit.

Row 32: Purl.

Row 33: Bind off 1 st, k20, bind off 1 st (22 sts).

Row 34: Purl.

Row 35: Knit.

Row 36: Bind off 1 st, p18, bind off 1 st (20 sts).

Row 37: Knit.

Row 38: Bind off 1 st, p16, bind off 1 st (18 sts).

Row 39: Bind off 1 st, k14, bind off 1 st (16 sts).

Row 40: Bind off 1 st, p12, bind off 1 st (14 sts).

Row 41: Bind off 1 st, k10, bind off 1 st (12 sts).

Row 42: Bind off 1 st, p8, bind off 1 st (10 sts).

Row 43: Bind off 1 st, k6, bind off 1 st (8 sts).

Row 44: Purl.

Bind off. Weave in ends.

Tab Closure

Hold two strands of yarn together throughout.

Cast on 9 sts.

Row 1: K1, *sl 1 wyif, move yarn to back and k1; rep from * to end.

Row 2 (RS): P2,*sl 1 wyib, move yarn to front and p1; rep from * to end.

Rows 3 and 4: Repeat Rows 1 and 2.

Row 5 (Make eyelet for twig closure): K1, sl 1 wyif, k1, k2tog, yo, sl 1 wyif, k1, sl 1 wyif, k1.

Row 6: Repeat Row 2.

Rows 7 – 38: Repeat Rows 1 and 2. Bind off. Weave in ends.

Assembling

Using the blunt tapestry needle and a single strand of silk yarn, sew the cast-on and bind-off edges of the bag body together. Remember that the purl side is the right side. Weave in ends.

Pin the bag bottom to the bag body with right sides together (purl side of bag body and knit side of bag bottom). Using the blunt tapestry needle and non-novelty yarn, sew these pieces together. Weave in ends.

(Optional): Turn bag right side out and position melamine board into place. If desired, this board can be covered with fabric.

Turn down 1½"/4cm of the top edge for the bag cuff. Set aside.

Preparing the Strap

Soak the grapevine branches in a bathtub or sink filled with water. Use whatever is handy to anchor them under water. Let them soak for one or two days or until they become flexible enough for shaping.

When the branches are ready for shaping, remove them from the water and shape them immediately. Entwine the branches so they act as one strap. Bend the branches in a curve and check the width (distance from one end of branches, straight across to the other end).

(Continued on next page)

Ooh—here's my pretty Fender Mustang. What a great color.

(Continued from previous page)

The width of the strap should correspond to the width of the bag. Check it against your bag to make sure. Use the fishing line to hold the branches in shape while they dry. Allow branches to dry thoroughly. This could take several days.

Apply polyurethane to the dried branches and the twig closure, and allow them to dry. Don't remove the fishing line yet.

Rehearsing in Kim's basement in Dayton, Ohio

Finishing

Attach the strap to the inside of the bag with fishing line. Because this can cause the inside of your bag to look messy, I used one strand of silk yarn to knit two rectangles large enough to cover the work inside. Use the fishing line or non-novelty yarn to tack these rectangles in place.

Pick the nicest side of the bag and, centered on the opposite side, sew the tab closure. As you sew, tack the bag cuff down as well.

Using the hammer and nail, or power hand drill, drill a small hole in the center of the twig closure. Using the blunt tapestry needle and silk yarn, sew the twig closure centered on the cuff of the nicer side of the bag. As you sew, tack the bag cuff down as well.

Remove the fishing line from the branches.

This Sari bag was knit with:

4 skeins of Sari Yarn, worsted weight, 100% recycled silk, 3.5oz/100g = approx 90yd/82m per skein, 2nd grade, multi-colors

Feedback

Sari silk yarn is made from the mill ends of saris collected from industrial mills in India. It's then handspun into yarn by women in South Asia. Second-grade silk yarn is coarser and has a variety of texture and color within each yard. These characteristics make it perfect for projects requiring body and structure.

Sari
REMIX

Here it is with a purchased wooden handle and a wooden bead.

Hey, Jute

RIFF

I know jute is rough on your hands, but this bag is worth it! It's indestructible, and the woven work on the strap makes it unique. You can use your scrap yarn for the weaving, but make sure it's chunky and single ply. The strap also serves as the bottom and sides of the bag.

FINISHED MEASUREMENTS

Height of Bag: 10"/25cm, excluding strap

Width of Bag: 10"/25cm

MATERIALS AND TOOLS

Color A: 180yd/165m of medium load twisted jute, jute, in natural

Color B: 284yd/260m of (4) worsted weight wool, merino/alpaca blend, in natural

125yd/114m of (5) chunky weight single-ply yarn, wool or wool blend, in yellow, light blue, aqua, navy, red, hunter green, gray and slate blue

Knitting needles: 6mm (size 10 U.S.), preferably metal

Blunt tapestry needle for sewing and weaving

2 pairs of gold, pronged magnetic snaps

Pliers to set snaps

1 felted swatch for inside pocket, approx 6"/15cm wide x 5"/13cm high, or any size desired (optional)

GAUGE

Exact gauge is not required for this project

Knitting

Side

(Make 2)

Hold one strand each of A and B together throughout.

Cast on 30 sts.

Rows 1 and 2: Knit.

Row 3: K1, p28, k1.

Row 4: Knit.

Rows 5 – 36: Repeat rows 3 and 4 sixteen times.

Bind off.

Making the Strap

Hold one strand each of A and B together throughout.

Cast on 6 sts.

Row 1: Knit.

Row 2: K1, p4, k1.

Repeat rows 1 and 2 until piece measures approx 67"/170cm.

Bind off.

Making the Tab Closure

Hold one strand each of A and B together throughout.

Cast on 6 sts.

Row 1: Knit.

Row 2: K1, p4, k1.

Repeat rows 1 and 2 until tab measures approx 7½"/19cm.

Bind off.

Feedback

Keep all your felted swatches; they make perfect patch pockets.

Weaving the Strap

Using a steam iron on magma (the hottest setting!), press the strap as flat as you can. This will stop the edges from rolling in and make the strap easier to weave.

Weaving begins at one end and is worked in 3½"/9cm rectangles across to the other end. Using the blunt tapestry needle and single-ply yarn, bring needle up between the Garter Stitch edge and the Stockinette Stitch section. Take the needle back down between the Stockinette Stitch section and the opposite Garter Stitch edge to complete one horizontal wrap. All weaving will be completed on the center Stockinette Stitch section, but not on the Garter Stitch edging. Work 15 – 20 horizontal wraps over a 3½"/9cm length of strap (figure 1).

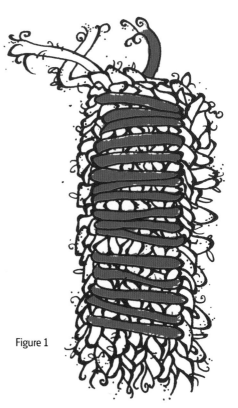

Figure 1

Use a contrasting color yarn and bring the needle up at one side of the rectangle halfway between the edges of the strap. Thread the needle under and over the horizontal wraps. I work from the center and complete one half then I start in the center again and complete the other half. Make sure you weave both the right side and the wrong side of the strap. As you work, use your needle to scrunch and tighten previous work (figure 2). Work 12 – 15 vertical weaves through each rectangle.

Weave in all ends.

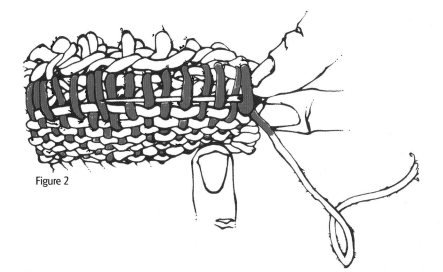

Figure 2

Weaving the Tabs

Weave a rectangle at each end of the tab in the same manner as the strap. The tab is approx 7"/18cm in length; work the rectangles over the first and last 2½"/6.4cm of the strap.

Finishing

Using a steam iron on hottest setting, press the sides of the bag as best you can. This makes it easier to work with them.

Using the blunt tapestry needle and one strand of B, sew short edges of strap together. Sew center of one long edge of strap around three edges of the front of the bag, centering joined end of strap along lower edge of front. Repeat to sew opposite long edge of strap around three edges of back of bag. Weave in ends.

One magnetic snap is attached to each end of the tab. This allows the tab to be lifted from either end. Position the male half of a snap in the woven area on the wrong side of the tab. Push the prongs through the weave and through the jute fabric, but not through the weave on the right side. Use pliers to bend the prongs and secure. Repeat with another male half of a snap on the other end of the tab. Position the female half of a snap on the right side of the front of the bag, centered about 1½"/4 cm from the top edge. Push the prongs through the jute fabric and slip the washer onto the prongs. Use pliers to bend the prongs and secure. Repeat with another female half of a snap on the back of the bag.

(Optional): Sew felt swatch to front or back of inside of bag to form a patch pocket.

This Hey, Jute bag was knit with:

Wellington Cordage's #14256 jute twine, 100% jute, 5oz/136g = approx 49yd/45m per ball

(A) 4 balls, natural

Bertagna Filati Aymara, worsted weight, 50% merino wool/50% super fine alpaca, 1.75oz/50g = approx 142yd/130m per ball, in natural

(B) 2 balls, #206

Manos del Uruguay's Wool, chunky weight, 100% wool, 3.5oz/100g = approx 135 yd/123m per hank, in #40 goldenrod, #C powder, #005 aqua, #011 navy, #66 poppy, #46 malachite, #F stone, and #29 steel

REMIX

...forget about making the bag and finishing it—just follow the instructions for making the strap and weaving it. Finally, you've found a good handmade guitar strap.

Turtleneck

RIFF

Alpaca felts like a dream. Now, I just need a sweater to match. The turtleneck can be folded deep or shallow, depending on what you like.

Making the Bag

FINISHED MEASUREMENTS (AFTER FELTING)

Height of Bag: 9½"/24cm, excluding strap

Width of Bag: 9½"/24cm

MATERIALS AND TOOLS

324yd/296m of ⑤ chunky weight yarn, alpaca, in fawn/cream

Knitting needles: 6 mm (size 10 U.S.), and 6 mm (size 10 U.S) circular needle, 16"/41cm long

Pins

Sharp tapestry needle

2.25mm (size B-1 U.S.) crochet hook

Stitch marker

Tan leather strap, 36"/91.5cm long

Assortment of glass beads, arranged into 18 groups

Beading needle or dental floss threader

Stretchy thread for beading

Sew-on snap closure

GAUGE

Exact gauge is not essential for this project.

Knitting

With A, cast on 44 sts. Leave a long tail for sewing.

Work in Stockinette Stitch (knit on RS, purl on WS) for 114 rows.

Bind off. Leave a long tail for sewing.

Finishing

With knit sides together, pin side edges in place. Using the sharp tapestry needle and long tails, sew side seams. Take an extra stitch or two on top edge of bag on each side. This will narrow the bag opening slightly.

Follow felting instructions on page 16 to felt bag.

Slip book into bag to block, and allow piece to dry.

Pick up and single crochet 72 stitches around the top edge of the bag. To do so, use crochet hook to pierce hole and pull yarn through, complete the crochet stitch, and repeat all around. Using circular needle, pick up and knit one stitch in each single crochet. Place stitch marker to mark beginning of round.

Work in k2, p2 rib for 37 rows. Bind off (not too tightly).

Using the sharp tapestry needle, sew the strap to the inside of the bag.

Assemble the bead groupings. Using the beading needle or dental floss threader (page 11) and stretchy cord, sew bead groupings evenly around bottom edge of the turtleneck.

Sew on the snap closure.

This Turtleneck bag was knit with:

3 skeins Misti's Alpaca, chunky weight, 100% baby alpaca, 3.5oz/100g = approx 108yd/99m per skein, color #469

Feedback

Here's a tip to pick up stitches evenly around your bag opening. Separate the opening into eight equal sections and mark it with pins. Divide the number of stitches to be picked up by the number of sections. For instance, this pattern calls for 72 stitches to be picked up. 72 divided by 8 equals 9. This means you need to pick up 9 stitches in each section.

Don't I look angry?
Who has my needles?!

Turtleneck

REMIX

For this bag I used contrasting color yarns for the turtleneck and the bag body. Also, I swapped the strap for one I knitted in Garter Stitch and then felted. Finally, I used glass beads for the bead groupings.

Recording

What's in the Bag?

Earplugs

9-volt batteries

Assortment of guitar and bass picks

Song lyrics and notes

Crossword puzzle

Aspirin

Nicotine gum

Knotted Up

RIFF

Because I'm rough on my handbags, this is one of my favorites. It's sturdy and roomy. If you haven't yet incorporated crochet into your knitting, this is your chance, since the panels are trimmed and joined with single crochet.

Making the Bag

FINISHED MEASUREMENTS (AFTER FELTING)

Height of Bag: 10½"/27cm, excluding strap

Width of Bag: 9"/23cm

Depth of Bag: 5"/13cm

MATERIALS AND TOOLS

Color A: 390yd/356m of (4) worsted weight yarn, wool, in green

Color B: 120yd/109m of (4) worsted weight yarn, wool, in brown

Knitting needles: 5.5 mm (size 9 U.S.)

Row counter (recommended)

4.5mm (size G-7 U.S.) crochet hook

Blunt tapestry needle for sewing

Pins

1 pair pronged, magnetic snap

GAUGE

Exact gauge is not essential for this project.

Knitting

Side/Strap Panel

(Make 2)

Beginning at lower end of panel, with A, cast on 16 sts.

Row 1: Knit.

Row 2: Pfb, p1, pfb, p1, pfb in next 7 sts, p1, pfb, p1, pfb, p1 (27 sts).

Rows 3 – 13: Work in Stockinette Stitch for 11 rows.

Row 14: P13, p2tog, p12 (26 sts).

Rows 15 – 22: Work in Stockinette Stitch for 8 rows.

Row 23: K12, k2tog, k12 (25 sts).

Rows 24 – 31: Work in Stockinette Stitch for 8 rows.

Row 32: P11, p2tog, p12 (24 sts).

Rows 33 – 40: Work in Stockinette Stitch for 8 rows.

Row 41: K11, k2tog, k11 (23 sts).

Rows 42 – 49: Work in Stockinette Stitch for 8 rows.

Row 50: P10, p2tog, p11 (22 sts).

Rows 51 – 58: Work in Stockinette Stitch for 8 rows.

Row 59: K10, k2tog, k10 (21 sts).

Rows 60 – 67: Work in Stockinette Stitch for 8 rows.

Row 68: P9, p2tog, p10 (20 sts).

Rows 69 – 76: Work in Stockinette Stitch for 8 rows.

Row 77: K9, k2tog, k9 (19 sts).

Rows 78 – 85: Work in Stockinette Stitch for 8 rows.

Row 86: P8, p2tog, p9 (18 sts).

Rows 87 – 103: Work in Stockinette Stitch for 17 rows.

Row 104: P8, p2tog, p8 (17 sts).

Rows 105 – 112: Work in Stockinette Stitch for 8 rows.

Row 113: K7, k2tog, k8 (16 sts).

Rows 114 – 121: Work in Stockinette Stitch for 8 rows.

Row 122: P7, p2tog, p7 (15 sts).

Rows 123 – 130: Work in Stockinette Stitch for 8 rows.

Row 131: K6, k2tog, k7 (14 sts).

Rows 132 – 139: Work in Stockinette Stitch for 8 rows.

Row 140: P6, p2tog, p6 (13 sts).

Rows 141 – 148: Work in Stockinette Stitch for 8 rows.

Row 149: K5, k2tog, k6 (12 sts).

Rows 150 – 157: Work in Stockinette Stitch for 8 rows.

Row 158: P5, p2tog, p5 (11 sts).

Rows 159 – 166: Work in Stockinette Stitch for 8 rows.

Singing with my boyfriends, The Supersuckers, at the Troubadour in Los Angeles

Row 167: K4, k2tog, k5 (10 sts).
Rows 168 – 175: Work in
    Stockinette Stitch for 8 rows.
Row 176: P4, p2tog, p4 (9 sts).
Rows 177 – 184: Work in
    Stockinette Stitch for 8 rows.
Row 185: K3, k2tog, k4 (8 sts).
Rows 186 – 193: Work in
    Stockinette Stitch for 8 rows.
Row 194: P3, p2tog, p3 (7 sts).
Rows 195 – 204: Work in
    Stockinette Stitch for 10 rows.
Row 205: K2tog, k5 (6 sts).
Rows 206 – 207: Work in
    Stockinette Stitch for 2 rows.
Row 208: P4, p2tog (5 sts).
Rows 209 – 210: Work in
    Stockinette Stitch for 2 rows.
Row 211: K2tog, k3 (4 sts).
Rows 212 – 213: Work in
    Stockinette Stitch for 2 rows.
Row 214: P2, p2tog (3 sts).
Row 215: Knit.
Row 216: P1, p2tog (2 sts).
Row 217: Knit.
Row 218: P2tog (1 st).
Bind off.

Front/Back Panel

(Make 2)
With A, cast on 21 sts.
Row 1: Knit.
Row 2: Pfb, p1, pfb, p1, pfb twice,
    p1, pfb in next 7 sts, p1, pfb
    twice, p1, pfb, p1, pfb (36 sts).
Rows 3 – 72: Work in Stockinette
    Stitch for 70 rows.
Bind off.

Bottom

With A, cast on 6 sts.
Row 1: Knit.
Row 2: Pfb, p4, pfb (8 sts).

(Continues on next page)

(Continued from previous page)

Row 3: Kfb, k6, kfb (10 sts).
Row 4: Purl.
Row 5: Kfb, k8, kfb (12 sts).
Rows 6 – 8: Work in Stockinette
    Stitch for 3 rows.
Row 9: Kfb, k10, kfb (14 sts).
Rows 10 – 13: Work in Stockinette
    Stitch for 4 rows.
Row 14: Pfb, p12, pfb (16 sts).
Rows 15 – 33: Work in Stockinette
    Stitch for 19 rows.
Row 34: P2tog, p12, p2tog (14 sts).
Row 35 – 38: Work in Stockinette
    Stitch for 4 rows.
Row 39: K2tog, k10, k2tog (12 sts).
Row 40 – 42: Work in Stockinette
    Stitch for 3 rows.
Row 43: K2tog, k8, k2tog (10 sts).
Row 44: Purl.
Row 45: K2tog, k6, k2tog (8 sts).
Row 46: P2tog, p4, p2tog (6 sts).
Bind off.

Trimming the Bag
Side/Strap Panels

With right side facing and using
the crochet hook, join B with a
slip stitch (page 20) in the edge of
row 1. Chain 1 (page 20), single
crochet (page 20) in edge of next
3 rows, skip one row, *single
crochet in edge of next 4 rows,
skip one row; repeat from * to top
of panel, work 3 single crochet in
topmost stitch; work single crochet
as established down other side
of panel. Fasten off and weave
in ends.

Front/Back Panels

With right side facing and using
the crochet hook, join B with a
slip stitch in the edge of row 1.
Chain 1, single crochet in edge of
each row to top right-hand corner,
work 3 single crochet in top right-
hand corner; single crochet in each
stitch across top of panel; work
3 single crochet in top left-hand
corner; single crochet in edge of
each row to lower edge of panel.
Fasten off and weave in ends.

Making the Knotted
Tab Closure

Select one of the front/back panel
pieces for the back of the bag.
With the right side facing, using
knitting needles and B, pick up
10 sts from the center top edge
of the crocheted trim. Work rows
170 – 218 of the Side/Strap Panel.
Using the crochet hook and B, trim
the tab in single crochet as in the
Side/Strap Panel trim directions.
Weave in ends.

Assembling

Hold wrong sides of one front/back
panel and one side/strap panel
together. Using the crochet hook
and B, working through both

thicknesses, slip stitch into the first
chain 1. Chain 1, single crochet
in each single crochet to top edge
of front/back panel. Repeat this
process to join all four corner edges
of bag. Weave in ends.

Turn bag inside out and pin bottom
piece in place. Using the tapestry
needle and A, sew bottom in place.
Weave in ends.

Finishing

Turn the bag right side out. Follow
the felting instructions on page 16
to felt the bag.

Using a steam iron on wool setting,
press the side sections that will
function as the straps, and the tab.
The crochet edging in the bag body
may also be pressed. Use an oven
mitt and place your hand in the
bag to provide resistance to the
iron. Don't lay the bag body flat
out to iron.

Knot the straps together at desired
length. Knot the end of tab.

Use plastic bags to gently shape bag
for blocking. Don't overstuff it. It
will lose its jaunty shape! Hang bag
to dry.

Attach magnetic snap to knotted
tab closure and bag body.

This Knotted Up bag was knit with:

Berroco's Peruvia, worsted weight,
100% Peruvian highland wool,
3.5oz/100g = approx 174yd/160m
per hank.

(A) 3 hanks, color #7122

(B) 1 hank, color #7123

Feedback

Need to press or block a bag but can't lay it flat?
Easy—put on an oven mitt and use your hand
as an ironing board. Just make sure the mitt is
really heat resistant!

Knotted Up

REMIX

Here it is in neutrals... very classy.

Only the front and back panels were knit in orange; everything else is in blue. This color combination gives the bag a hippy look.

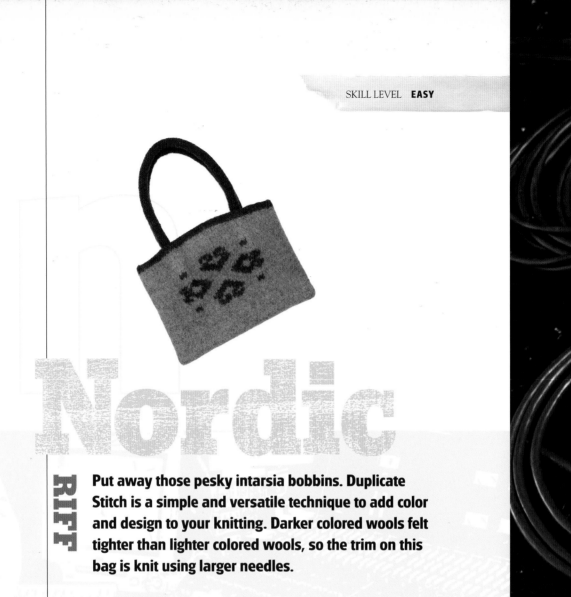

Nordic

RIFF

Put away those pesky intarsia bobbins. Duplicate Stitch is a simple and versatile technique to add color and design to your knitting. Darker colored wools felt tighter than lighter colored wools, so the trim on this bag is knit using larger needles.

Making the Bag

FINISHED MEASUREMENTS (AFTER FELTING)

Height of Bag: 8"/20cm, excluding strap

Width of Bag: 11"/28cm

MATERIALS AND TOOLS

Color A: 220yd/201m of (4) worsted weight yarn, wool, in light brown

Color B: 220yd/201m of (4) worsted weight yarn, wool, in dark brown

Color C: 2yd/2m of (4) worsted weight yarn, wool, in coral

Knitting needles: 4.5 mm (size 7 U.S.) and 5.5 mm (size 9 U.S.)

Blunt tapestry needle for embroidery

Pins

Sharp tapestry needle for sewing

Large safety pin, size 3

1½yd/1.4m poly cord upholstery piping 7/16"/11mm diameter

Sew-on snap closure

GAUGE

Exact gauge is not essential for this project.

Knitting

Using larger needles and B, cast on 49 sts.

Work in Stockinette Stitch for 4 rows.

Change to smaller needles and A.

Work in Stockinette Stitch for 141 rows.

Change back to larger needles and B.

Work in Stockinette Stitch for 4 rows.

Bind off.

Assembling

Using a steam iron on wool setting, press the edges of the bag to prevent rolling. This will make it easier to work with.

Using the blunt tapestry needle, Duplicate Stitch (page 21) the Nordic Design (figure 1). Weave in all ends.

Fold bag in half with knit sides together, bringing the cast-on edge up to meet the bind-off edge. Pin edges together. Using the sharp tapestry needle and matching color yarn, sew edges together. Weave in ends.

Making the Straps

(Make 2)

Using smaller needles and B, cast on 9 sts. Leave long tail for sewing.

Work in Stockinette Stitch for 120 rows.

Bind off. Leave long tail for sewing.

|O| —This stitch represents the center of the motif and should be embroidered on the 25th stitch of the 33rd row.

x—Color B

o—Color C

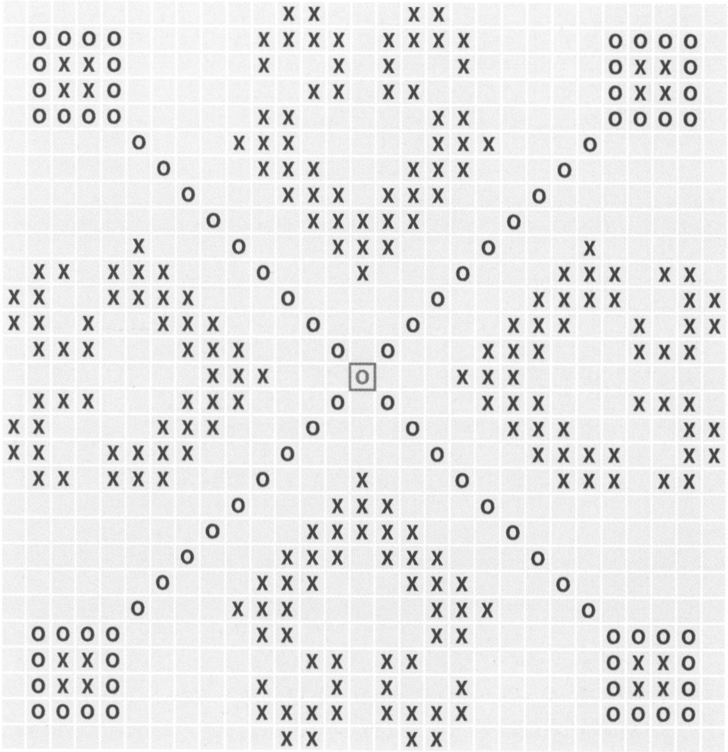

Figure 1

Assembling the Straps

Using long tails, sew edges together to form tubes. *Tip:* Use a large knitting needle to wrap the edges around as you sew. Weave in ends.

Finishing

Follow the felting instructions on page 16 to felt the bag and straps.

Slip a book into the bag to block. Gently pull the centers of the opening edges of the bag body, to shape a curve in the center top, and allow the bag to dry.

Using the large safety pin, thread upholstery piping through felted tubes and allow them to dry.

Trim the excess piping and sew the ends of each tube closed. Weave in ends.

Pin the strap ends in place on the inside of the bag. Using the sharp tapestry needle and B, sew strap ends in place. Weave in ends.

Sew on snap closure.

This Nordic bag was knit with:

Cascade Yarns' 220, worsted weight, 100% wool, 3.5oz/100g = approx 220yd/201m per skein

(A) 1 skein, color #4010

(B) 1 skein, color #9459

(C) 1 skein, color #7830

Feedback

If the ends of your upholstery piping are frayed, wrap tape tightly around the ends. Attach the safety pin through the taped area and feed it through the tube.

Nordic REMIX

If there are no brown M&Ms allowed backstage, carry this bag instead. It's knit in dark and light forest greens with hot pink detail.

Trixie Delicious

RIFF

Yes—another easy bag that knits up quickly in Garter Stitch! Check the width at the cast-on and bind-off edges of your knitted fabric to make sure your frame fits. There's such a variety of handbag hardware available now. Frames are easy to use and really make your bag look pro.

FINISHED MEASUREMENTS

Height of Bag: 6½"/17cm, excluding strap

Width of Bag: 6½"/17cm

MATERIALS AND TOOLS

Color A: 176yd/160m of ④ worsted weight eyelash yarn, polyester/rayon/acrylic/polyamide blend, in multi-colors

Color B: 82yd/74m of ③ DK yarn, cotton, in black

Knitting needles: 4mm (size 6 U.S.), preferably metal, or size to obtain gauge

Purse frame, 5"/13cm wide x 3"/8cm high, excluding snap closure, and 5½"/14cm wide when fully open

Blunt tapestry needle for sewing

2 gold split key rings, ¾"/20mm

Gold chain, approx 36"/91cm

GAUGE

16 sts and 26 rows = 4"/10cm in Garter Stitch (knit every row), with two strands of A and one strand of B held together.

Always take time to check your gauge.

Knitting

Hold two strands of A and one strand of B together throughout.

Cast on 19 sts., leaving a long tail for sewing.

Rows 1 – 7: Knit.

Cut the yarn leaving a tail to secure and weave in later.

Row 8: Cast on 4 sts onto the free needle; k19 sts on the other needle (23 sts). Cut the yarn leaving a tail to secure and weave in later. Cast on 4 sts onto the same needle; (27 sts), leaving a long tail for sewing.

Rows 9 – 87: Knit.

Row 88: Bind off 4 sts, k19, bind off 4 sts (19 sts).

Cut the yarn leaving a long tail to secure and weave in later.

Rows 89 – 94: Knit.

Bind off leaving a long tail for sewing. Weave in all ends.

Finishing

Slip the edge of the knitted fabric over the frame rod and under the frame edge. Using the blunt tapestry needle and B, sew the edge to the inside of the bag. Repeat this process for the other side of the frame.

Flip the bag inside out. Starting at the bottom, sew one side together for about 4"/10cm; do not cut the yarn. Repeat for the other side.

Flip the bag right side out. Fold the top, open portion of the sides of the fabric over the bag frame sides and sew. Make sure to check that the bag frame will still close! Do not sew fabric over the frame hinge. Weave in all ends.

Attach the key rings to the frame strap loops. Attach the chain to the key rings.

This Trixie Delicious bag was knit with:

Filatura Di Crosa's Brazil, worsted weight, 47% polyester/44% rayon/8% acrylic/1% polyamide, 1.75oz/50g = approx 88yd/80m per ball.

(A) 2 balls, color #108

Classic Elite's Provence, DK weight, 100% mercerized cotton, 3.5oz/100g = approx 205yd/186m per skein.

(B) 1 skein, color #2613

Feedback

If your eyelash loses its fluff, gently brush the bag with a soft bristled brush to coax the eyelash up and out.

REMIX

Because the frame has built-in rings, it's a cinch to swap out handles.

I can't remember where this was taken, but my hair looks really good.

Graffiti

RIFF

This bag is an example of where knitting is today. No longer confined to dusty afghans and T.P. cozies, it has evolved into wearable art. Although the techniques required for this pattern are easy, I rate it slightly more challenging because of the amount of embroidery involved.

FINISHED MEASUREMENTS (AFTER FELTING)

Height of Bag: 9"/23cm, excluding strap

Width of Bag: 11"/28cm

MATERIALS AND TOOLS

Color A: 220yd/201m of ④ worsted weight yarn, wool, in light gray

Color B: 75yd/69m of ④ worsted weight yarn, wool, in yellow

Color C: 62yd/57m of ④ worsted weight yarn, wool, in red

Color D: 62yd/57m of ④ worsted weight yarn, wool, in light blue

Color E: 9yd/7m of ④ worsted weight yarn, wool, in dark purple

Knitting needles: 5mm (size 8 U.S.)

Blunt tapestry needle for embroidery

Sharp tapestry needle for sewing and embroidery

Wire cutters or scissors

Bass guitar string, medium gauge, low E

2 large crimps or splice caps, any color

Pliers or crimpers

Clear fishing line to sew strap ends to bag (or just use project yarn)

Black washable marker

Sew-on snap closure

GAUGE

Exact gauge is not essential for this project.

Knitting

With A, cast on 55 sts.
Work in Stockinette Stitch for 136 rows.
Bind off.

Assembling

Using a steam iron on wool setting, press the edges of the bag to prevent rolling. This will make it easier to work with.

Using the blunt tapestry needle and the indicated colors, embroider the Graffiti Design (figure 2, pages 118 and 119) with Duplicate Stitch (page 21) and Split Stitch (page 21). Add bubbles as desired. Weave in all ends.

Fold bag in half with knit sides together, bringing the cast-on edge up to meet the bind-off edge. Using the sharp tapestry needle and A, sew side edges together. Weave in ends.

Preparing the Strap

Using wire cutters or scissors, trim the ends of the guitar string. You will be working with just the wire.

Fold the end of the wire approx 1½"/3.8cm from end, creating a loop. Pinch the loop in place. Slip the loop through the crimp to the end of the looped wire and, using pliers or crimper, crimp in place. See page 15 for photograph of assembly. Repeat on other end of guitar string.

Finishing

Follow the felting instructions on page 16 to felt the bag.

Slip a book into the bag to block and allow it to dry.

Using clear fishing line or matching project yarn, sew the strap edges to the inside side seams approx 4"/10cm down from the top edge of the bag. Weave in ends.

Using the marker, copy the signatures from the Kelp Signature Template (figure 1, page 117), or if you prefer, create your own tags and shout outs.

Using the sharp tapestry needle and E, embroider the Kelp signature with Split Stitch and the TM7 and KD with Back Stitch (page 21).

Sew on snap closure.

This Graffiti bag was knit with:

Cascade Yarn's 220, worsted weight, 100% wool, 3.5oz/100g = approx 220yd/201m per skein.

(A) 1 skein, color #8509

(B) 1 skein, color #7828

(C) 1 skein, color #8414

(D) 1 skein, color #7815

(E) 1 skein, color #8886

Feedback

What's it all mean? This graffiti artist goes by the moniker KELP. TM7 and KD are initials that accompany a tag or piece (short for "masterpiece") and signify crew or group affiliations. TM7, the abbreviation for "The Magnificent Seven," is named for the proximity of its founder to the 7 line of the New York transit system. KD is short for "Kids Destroy" (later changed to "Kings Destroy"), a Bronx-based crew. It was named by its founder, Cope2. The arrows and clouds used in the design are traditional elements of graffiti. Go online to see more of this artist's work.

Figure 1

REMIX

Tap into your inner vandal to create a different color palette. The strap used here is a thrift store belt.

Figure 2

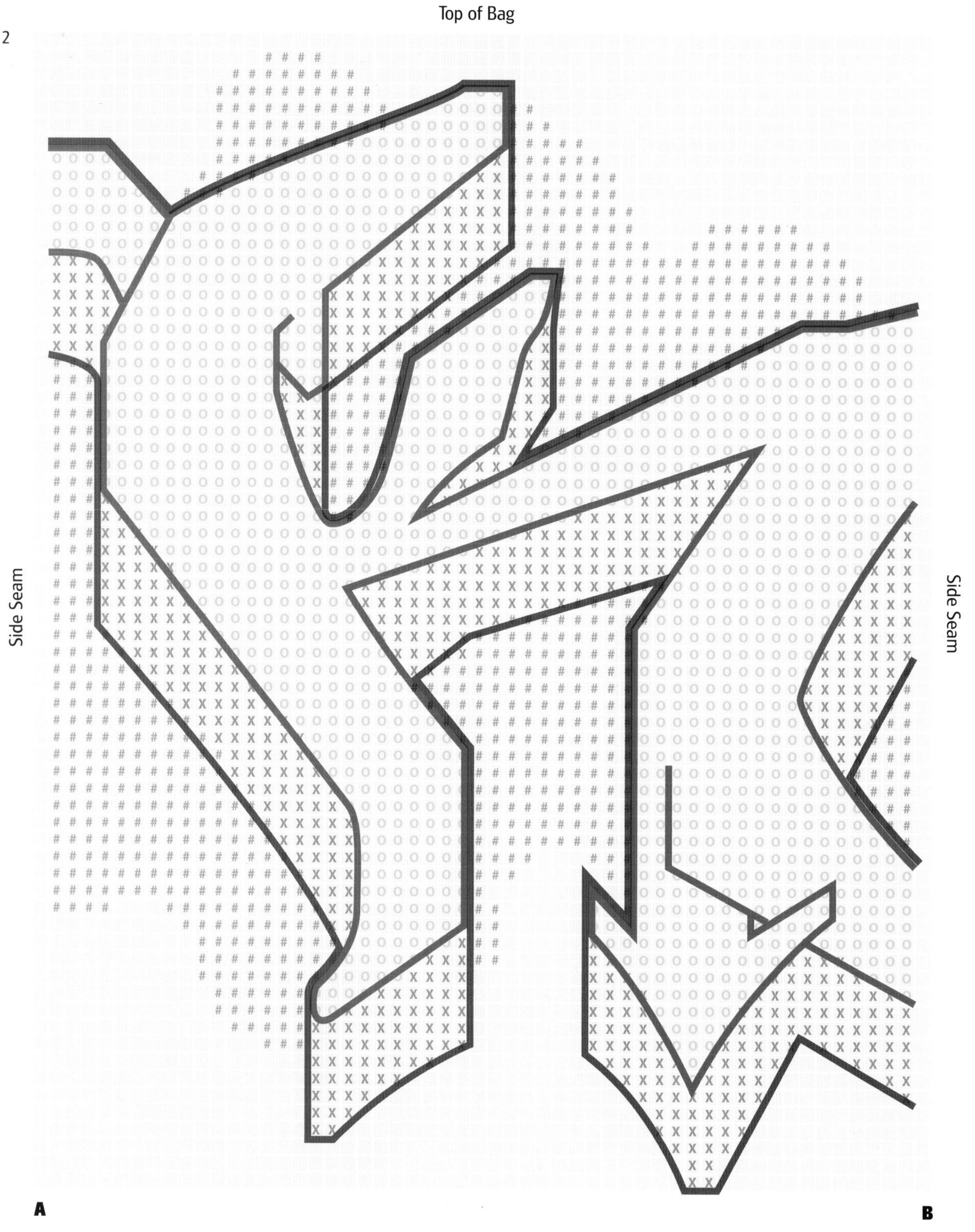
Top of Bag
Side Seam
Side Seam
A
B

To make the embroidery template, copy each of the halves shown above, cut them out, and tape them together, matching the spots marked A and B.

A

B

Side Seam

Side Seam

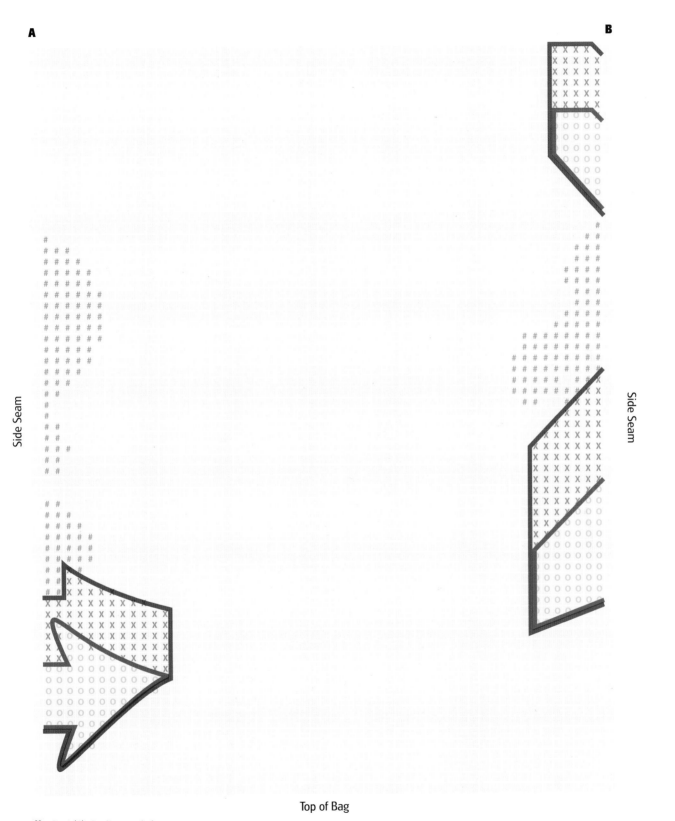

Top of Bag

X   Red (C) duplicate stitch
○   Yellow (B) duplicate stitch
Light blue (D) duplicate stitch
▬   Red (C) split stitch
▬   Purple (E) split stitch

Appendix

ABBREVIATIONS

dec	decrease
dpn	double pointed needle(s)
inc	increase
k	knit
kfb	knit in front and back
k2tog	knit two stitches together
k2tog tbl	knit two stitches together through back loops
m1	make one
p	purl
pfb	purl in front and back
p2tog	purl two stitches together
p2tog tbl	purl two stitches together through back loops
RS	right side
sl	slip
ssk	slip, slip, knit
st(s)	stitch(es)
WS	wrong side
wyib	with yarn in back
wyif	with yarn in front

YARN WEIGHT SYMBOL & CATEGORY NAMES	0 lace	1 super fine	2 fine	3 light	4 medium	5 bulky	6 super bulky
TYPE OF YARNS IN CATEGORY	Fingering, 10-count crochet thread	Sock, Fingering, Baby	Sport, Baby	DK, Light Worsted	Worsted, Afghan, Aran	Chunky, Craft, Rug	Bulky, Roving

Source: Craft Yarn Council of America's www.YarnStandards.com

CROCHET HOOK EQUIVALENTS

Depending on the material and the manufacturer, several different numbering systems exist for crochet hook sizes. The only constant measurement scale is the metric system, which is often included alongside the size indicator on each hook.

US Size	Metric
B-1	2.25 mm
C-2	2.75 mm
D-3	3.25 mm
E-4	3.50 mm
F-5	3.75 mm
G-6	4.00 mm
7	4.50 mm
H-8	5.00 mm
I-9	5.50 mm
J-10	6.00 mm
K-10 1/2	6.50 mm
L-11	8.00 mm
M/N-13	9.00 mm
N/P-15	10.00 mm

ACKNOWLEDGMENTS

I'd like to thank my husband, Todd Mund, for his sweet encouragement and for keeping his eyes from glazing over whenever I mentioned the words "my book."

When I taped an episode of DIY network's *Knitty Gritty* with Vickie Howell, the producers asked me, "Where's your book?" I answered, "Good question. Where *is* my book?" Vickie told me, "Don't worry, we'll fix that." And she did. My thanks to Vickie for making this book happen and for making me feel that I could call her *anytime* for advice. Because I did!

The artist Chris Glass gave generously of his time to help me shape this book. He's a creative wizard who showed me how cool this book could look. His work helped me understand mine.

I'm not a writer, but my editor, Suzanne Tourtillott, made me sound like I am. Many thanks to Suzanne for holding my hand and guiding me through the process. Thanks also to Kay J. Hay for her careful technical edit of the text. I appreciate the people who helped keep tabs on the many different elements involved in creating this book: Kathleen McCafferty, Nathalie Mornu, Beth Sweet, and editorial intern Halley Lawrence.

I'd like to thank this book's art director, Kristi Pfeffer, for her enthusiasm and her willingness to try something different. Thanks to photographer Stewart O'Shields and his assistant Megan Cox for the beautiful shots of the bags. Thanks to models Amanda Carestio, Megan Cox, Kara Helmkamp, Robb Helmkamp, Avery Johnson, Tess Redlinger, Beth Sweet, Hannah Waldrop, and Shannon Yokeley. Thanks also to Jeff Hamilton and Avery Johnson for their art production help, and to Orrin Lundgren and Eva Reitzel for the illustrations.

Thanks to Kyle Rector for his contribution to the Graffiti Bag and for patiently explaining the mysteries of the graffiti world.

Thanks to everyone who contributed their photos and images to this book: Mando Lopez, Ed Horrox, Andrea Campos, Chris Glass, everyone at 4AD, Jonathan Furmanski, Maria Paneres, and Vater Percussion.

Lastly, I'd like to thank my sister, Kim Deal, for being at my beck and call while I was writing this book, and for spending hours on late-night phone calls with me—just listening. She typed, embroidered, and even learned to knit for me!

Photo Credits
Andrea Campos, pages 18, 65, 79, 102
Kim Deal, pages 56, 126
Chris Glass, pages 7, 8, 29, 36, 44, 46, 51, 75, 85, 87, 88, 90, 96, 111
Ed Horrox, pages 14, 25, 70, 98, 101
Mando Lopez, pages 10, 11, 15, 16, 17, 33, 41, 54, 61, 106, 115
Todd Mund, pages 9, 12, 13, 113

ABOUT THE AUTHOR

Kelley Deal is a guitarist and vocalist for the multi-platinum selling band, The Breeders. They have been on MTV, the *Late Show with David Letterman*, *Late Night with Conan O'Brien*, and *Buffy the Vampire Slayer*, among numerous other television appearances.

Kelley is a functioning knit-o-holic whose knitted creations have been sold in boutiques across the United States and have also been featured in various magazines, as well as appearing on the DIY network's craft show, *Knitty Gritty*.

Kelley's unusual experiences inspire her knitting. When on the road, she visits yarn stores in countries like Iceland, Australia, and Chile, and often has yarn thrown to her onstage. Music and a lifestyle of touring collide with tangled yarn and needles to create a venue where she might knit with drumsticks and recycle old guitar strings for handbag straps.

INDEX

A NOTE ABOUT SUPPLIERS

Having trouble finding supplies? We've created a listing of suppliers on our website, which we update on a regular basis. Visit us at www.larkbooks.com, click on "Sources," and then search for the relevant topic. You will find numerous companies listed, with the web address and/or mailing address and phone number.

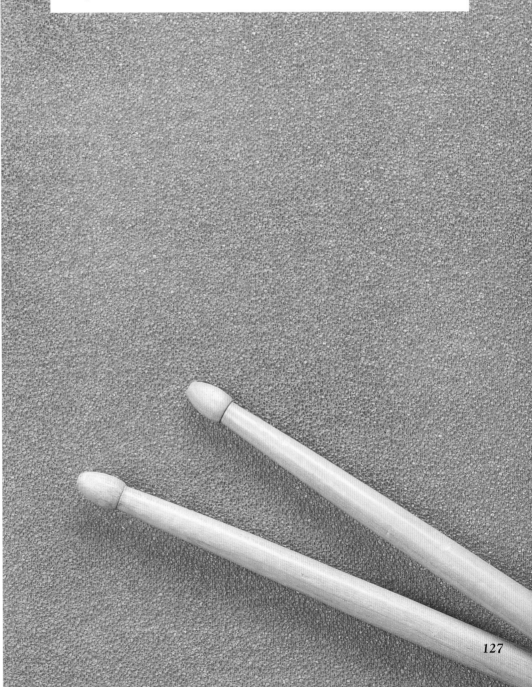